THE FAMILY ALSO NEEDS PRUNING

LUIS FERNANDO RODRIGO VALLEBONA

HOW TO AVOID FAMILY ENVY, CYNICISM, AND HARM

CONTENTS

DISCLAIMER

The information contained in this publication is provided for reference purposes only. Neither the author, nor the publisher, nor any person involved in the production of this book is responsible for the use that each reader makes of the information or for the results arising from their actions.

This book is dedicated to my wife and my children.

OPENING WORDS

In the human fabric of a family, closeness does not automatically guarantee honesty or goodwill. We have been taught to believe that family is synonymous with unconditional unity, that the mere fact of sharing blood or a last name is enough to warrant total devotion, blind loyalty, and automatic forgiveness. That idea, repeated generation after generation, is rarely questioned, which is why it is so difficult to put into words what happens when it falls short.

This book draws on that everyday experience to explore a real and subtle phenomenon: the exploitation of closeness by certain relatives who act out of interests that do not always align with the well-being of the family unit. Far from fostering mistrust, it offers a clear analysis of recurring dynamics and signs that, when taken together, reveal a pattern capable of eroding trust and family cohesion.

The aim is to provide tools for distinguishing between genuine affection and affection used as a bargaining chip, thereby protecting everyone's emotional well-being.

The book identifies patterns that often go unnoticed when viewed as isolated gestures—whether they are conditional favors, selective praise intended to elicit something in return, criticism disguised as good intentions, complicit silence in the face of questionable behavior, or an emotional investment that favors one party while undermining the others.

Also featured are ambiguity, used as a tactic to buy time or avoid commitments; and guilt, employed to justify demands or impose narratives. Rather than pointing fingers, these elements reveal a mosaic of behaviors that, when repeated, expose a logic of control or influence capable of damaging the emotional network.

Throughout these pages, you will find a practical guide that combines careful observation, assertive communication, and clear boundaries. You are also encouraged to identify patterns over time, demand consistency between words and actions, listen with empathy, and ask direct questions to clarify intentions. This book emphasizes the need to document relevant interactions, seek support from neutral third parties when necessary, and diversify one's support network to avoid dangerous dependencies. Self-care and emotional protection emerge as pillars of firm boundaries, responsible decisions, and a healthy flow of affection that sustains personal autonomy without fracturing relationships.

The mission is to strengthen nurturing bonds, educate new generations in an ethical understanding of relationships, and provide a framework for acting with courage and compassion when reality becomes difficult.

These pages serve as a compass to navigate the complexity of family emotions with clarity, and as an invitation to build a more authentic, more responsible coexistence capable of enduring over time, even in the face of inevitable tensions. With this purpose in mind, the book guides the reader, chapter by chapter, toward a more humane and wiser family life.

INTRODUCTION TO FALSE RELATIVES

Not all close bonds turn out to be genuine, and this is something we must clearly acknowledge, especially within the human fabric of a family. Although we have historically been led to believe that closeness as relatives automatically breeds honesty and good intentions, in this chapter we will explore the term "false relative."

This term has been used to describe a person who, despite being part of the family circle or presenting themselves as such, acts out of interests that do not align with the well-being of the family unit. It should be noted that this is not a call for indiscriminate mistrust; rather, it is a strategic analysis of the dynamics that, over time, can erode trust, mutual support, and the family's ability to sustain itself in times of difficulty.

Identifying these dynamics requires carefully observing patterns that recur; these are signs that, taken in isolation, might go unnoticed, but which, taken together, reveal a direction that does not serve the family's unity.

The definition of a "false relative" is based, above all, on the observation of behaviors that persist over time and reveal a discrepancy between the affection expressed and the actions expected in a truly reciprocal relationship.

Among these traits are conditional favors, compliments that seem to boost self-esteem only when they benefit the other party, or criticism presented as well-intentioned advice but which, at its core, seeks to shape decisions or control narratives.

It is also common to encounter complicit silence in the face of inappropriate behavior, a disproportionate emotional investment that seems to favor one party while simultaneously disparaging or dismissing other members when they do not serve a specific purpose.

In social contexts, these dynamics can translate into discreet alliances to gain influence, symbolic gains, or access to resources; and within the family, into a subtle erosion that undermines trust among siblings, cousins, or parents and adult children.

Recognizing the presence of these dynamics does not imply a catastrophic view of the family; however, it can signal the beginning of a clearer perspective. By understanding who brings real value to the relationship and which bonds sustain the emotional network, it becomes possible to prioritize healthy connections and protect oneself from manipulations that, over time, can leave scars that are difficult to heal.

Encouraging the identification of these patterns stems from the need to preserve the emotional well-being and cohesion of the family unit, because when relationships are distorted by hidden agendas, the cost is high and accumulates over time.

Furthermore, conflicts resurface with the same intensity, resentments persist far beyond a single incident, and a sense of betrayal can take root in family gatherings and shared memories.

Therefore, it is helpful to map out typical behaviors and triggers that fuel mistrust, with the goal of anticipating tensions and making more informed decisions about where to invest time, energy, and boundaries.

This book proposes a practical path for addressing the complexity of these dynamics with empathy and determination—by listening attentively without being swayed by empty praise, noticing when reciprocity is conditional, and recognizing that offered support appears only at convenient moments. These practices enable us to distinguish between genuine affection and maneuvers designed to gain advantages at the expense of the truth.

It also distinguishes between sympathy and responsibility; the former can be misleading, while the latter requires a conscious acceptance of boundaries, taking responsibility for one's own mistakes, and not shifting inevitable blame onto others. The aim is to empower, not to assign blame, and to equip each reader with tools to build a network of emotional connections that fosters mutual growth, shared responsibility, and emotional autonomy within the family.

> Clarity about the intentions of those around us becomes a central skill for sustaining nurturing human bonds, even in the face of inevitable tensions.

To better understand the definition and scope of this phenomenon, it is helpful to consider examples that frequently occur in family settings, without resorting to extreme cases or situations detached from everyday reality. Let's imagine a cousin who arrives at a gathering and, with expressions of great warmth, offers help with a personal project in exchange for a promise of future loyalty in sensitive decisions. On the surface, the help seems selfless, but upon closer examination of the context, it becomes clear that the true "monetization" of the relationship occurs through favors requested later and through praise that intensifies when the matter benefits that person.

Another common pattern is the use of guilt by someone who points out a supposed rift when another person does not accept a demand, emphasizing that "the family should be united" and then presenting the pressure to comply with certain wishes as proof of affection.

Ambiguity is also an ally of manipulation, as it involves vague promises, changing stories depending on the audience, and a series of narratives designed to influence the family's collective memory. In social media and social circles, the figure of the "strategic ally" may emerge—someone who, in front of the cameras, supports everyone, but in private fuels rumors or skews information to favor a specific narrative.

These behaviors, when repeated regularly, erode trust and create a climate in which the truth can become buried under a layer of convenient interpretations.

The scope of these phenomena is broad because they are not limited to a single type of relationship or a single part of the home; furthermore, they can arise in the dynamics between adult siblings competing for recognition, between cousins seeking influence over future decisions, or between parents and children when there are disputes over decisions involving resources, care, or legacies.

In a more subtle way, it can manifest itself in the way news is reported; for example, one version is presented to win sympathy, while another is kept hidden to prevent certain interests from being questioned.

The key here is consistency between words and actions over time, the ability to listen and have difficult conversations without seeking an advantage, and the openness to admit mistakes when they occur.

These conditions point to a relationship that can be sustained with authenticity, even amid tensions, because when they are not met, there is a greater risk of perpetuating dynamics that erode the family's trust and emotional security. In practical terms, recognizing a false relative requires a broad yet rigorous perspective:

- **Broad**: This involves observing face-to-face interactions, the underlying messages, the demands hidden behind apparent kindness, and the pattern of responses to conflicts.
- **Rigorous:** This involves distinguishing between isolated signals and a set of clues that point to a clear objective of influencing, controlling, obtaining benefits, or diverting resources.

The tools for this analysis are not intended to turn the family into a laboratory of suspicion, but rather to enable each member to make informed decisions about their level of trust, the degree of closeness they are willing to maintain, and the boundaries they need to establish to protect their well-being.

In this regard, intuition plays a valuable role, always honed by experience, repeated observation, and shared reflection when the family comes together to discuss how they feel about certain behaviors or decisions.

To clarify the central idea, it is helpful to imagine a simple mental framework—one that distinguishes between affection that is sustained for its own sake and affection that functions as a bargaining chip.

When people behave as if everything were natural and unconditional, the bond flows naturally; when, even while present, they impose conditions or perpetuate a narrative that benefits one party, the bond is overshadowed by self-interest.

This framework does not aim to oversimplify human complexity or rule out the possibility of legitimate moments of tension within the family; on the contrary, it seeks to provide a compass to guide decisions when such tensions arise and to protect the emotional well-being of those within the family network.

Ultimately, understanding what a "false relative" is and what their presence entails opens the door to a more mindful way of living together, in which bonds that support the growth, trust, and dignity of each member are prioritized—without ignoring the need for clear boundaries and shared responsibility for safeguarding the emotional well-being of the family as a whole.

The definition and scope of "false relatives" are set within a reality that, though painful at at times, offers an opportunity for learning and growth.

Recognizing and naming these dynamics is the first step toward building a more authentic emotional network—one capable of withstanding challenges, resisting the temptation to force loyalty at the expense of truth, and upholding, with courage and empathy, the common well-being.

This approach allows us to move toward a more transparent family relationship, where each member's emotional freedom is respected and where shared responsibility becomes the foundation of a way of living together that honors everyone's dignity.

Ultimately, clarity about what is authentic and what is not does not sever human bonds; rather, it strengthens them when accompanied by healthy boundaries, open communication, and an ongoing commitment to the family's emotional well-being.

Encouraging the identification of "false relatives" stems from a deep need to protect the family's emotional health and cohesion in the face of dynamics that, whether through discretion or repetition, ultimately erode everyone's trust and well-being.

When family relationships are distorted by hidden agendas, the cost is significant; the effects manifest as recurring conflicts, accumulated resentments, and a sense of betrayal that eventually seeps into gatherings, everyday conversations, and the memory of shared experiences.

Identifying these dynamics early on does not mean succumbing to mistrust; rather, it means gaining the strategic clarity needed to decide where to invest time, energy, and boundaries, and to prioritize bonds that sustain the family's authenticity.

The motivation to identify these dynamics does not stem from a desire to point fingers; it arises from a commitment to a family environment where affection and responsibility go hand in hand. Sometimes, the presence of a supposedly close bond can mask a personal agenda that does not prioritize the collective well-being. On other occasions, the presence of praise, favors, or apparent gestures of closeness acts as a mask that hides decisions that benefit only one party.

Understanding these tensions and recognizing their recurrence over time allows each family member to place these signals within a broader context, because not everything that appears to be affection is necessarily selfless support, and not every instance of distance or reserve is a betrayal.

The goal is to provide tools for distinguishing between what nurtures and what wears us down, so that the network of relationships can be strengthened through clarity and shared responsibility. Let's observe how these patterns manifest in daily life, since one of the key elements is the recurrence of behaviors that appear time and again, so that, over time, they become predictable.

- **Conditional favors:** someone offers support or provides benefits only when certain conditions are met that ensure a future gain for them.
- **Selective praise:** words of praise offered when seeking to influence a decision or win a favor, while disregarding the legitimacy of such recognition when circumstances do not serve one's interests.
- **Complicit silence in the face of inappropriate behavior:** the failure to point out or correct behaviors that, if reported, could disrupt a narrative that favors a specific party; and, at the same time, a constant emotional investment that disproportionately favors one's own interests, leaving others with less space to express their own needs.

In social and family contexts, these dynamics can take more subtle forms, such as discreet alliances to gain influence, strategic distractions to divert attention from a real conflict, or a kind of gradual erosion that undermines trust among siblings, cousins, or adult children.

Recognizing their existence, as already mentioned, is not about passing judgment in advance or diagnosing permanent betrayals; rather, it is about opening the door to a more realistic understanding of the emotional network that sustains the family—identifying who truly provides stable support, who demonstrates consistency between their words and actions, and who tends to act out of interests that do not align with mutual care.

The central motivation, then, is directed toward a practical and humane goal: to build a framework of healthier relationships, where the authenticity of affection stands in contrast to attempts at manipulation.

This framework does not seek to abruptly tear the family apart, but rather to teach how to distinguish between bonds that nourish and those that, even when close, function as instruments of power or control. To this end, it is crucial to understand that identification is not a witch hunt; it is a discipline of observation and decision-making that involves listening attentively and discerning between praise that strengthens and promises that mask personal gain.

In turn, it means recognizing when reciprocity is genuine and when listening is conditioned by a hidden agenda; it also involves identifying the difference between sympathy and responsibility, because sympathy may stem from good intentions, but responsibility is required when someone's actions affect the well-being of the family unit.

This book offers a practical path for exploring these issues with empathy and clarity, since empathy is not a substitute for vigilance; rather, it is balanced by a critical eye that remains open to discordant signals.

It is important to note that listening with an open mind—but without being swayed by empty praise or ambiguous promises—becomes a core skill; and observing when reciprocity appears authentically, or when help comes only at convenient times, becomes a habit that guides decision-making.

On the other hand, recognizing the difference between sympathy and responsibility allows us, for example, to distinguish between a phone call offering comfort during a crisis and a support network that remains available even when there is no explicit benefit.

The motivation to identify these distinctions also involves an invitation to evaluate one's own behavior, because each person, by looking inward, can ask themselves whether they are contributing to a climate of trust or, on the contrary, replicating patterns that foster control or dependence.

Recognizing one's own mistakes, taking responsibility when appropriate, and correcting courses of action are key components of a more mature way of living together.

In this sense, identification is a practice of personal and collective responsibility, since when a family strengthens its ability to honestly evaluate its dynamics, conditions are created for shared growth to have a more solid foundation.

The approach proposed in this chapter is neither rigid nor dogmatic; it is not about drawing up a list of faults or labeling each family member as "insincere" based on a single isolated experience. Rather, it is about developing practical guidelines for observing with patience, communicating clearly, and making decisions based on what best serves the long-term well-being of the family as a whole. Being aware of these dynamics also creates opportunities for new generations to learn to distinguish between genuine affection and utilitarianism.

Through the emotional education suggested here, children and young people can understand that family love cannot be bought or imposed; it is cultivated through healthy boundaries, honest conversations, and a framework of shared responsibility.

This is a central theme that, within the book's framework, ensures continuity across generations in fostering emotional autonomy within the family without sacrificing closeness or a sense of belonging.

Ultimately, the goal is to empower:

- The ability to clearly identify when a relationship is nurturing and when, on the contrary, it is draining.
- To be able to calmly decide where to invest energy, set boundaries, and allocate time.
- The ability to distinguish between a word of encouragement that strengthens and criticism that, disguised as concern, seeks to assert a position.

- The ability to maintain hope for authentic connections while setting boundaries that protect each person's well-being and, at the same time, the balance of the family as a whole.

This balance is not static and requires conscious vigilance, open communication, and an ongoing commitment to shared truth. As a person internalizes these ideas, their understanding of family dynamics becomes less ambiguous and more manageable. Patterns that, at first glance, may seem inevitable or natural lose their sense of inevitability and become challenges that can be addressed with concrete tools—such as behavioral maps, direct questions, clear boundaries, and emotional support that leaves no one behind but also does not condone abuse or manipulation.

The motivation to identify these patterns, therefore, is an invitation to build a network of relationships that sustains the family in adversity and, at the same time, preserves the dignity of each member.

This path does not exclude the complexity of emotions or the difficulty of family situations.

> Recognizing that certain dynamics—no matter how familiar they may be—require reevaluation, correction, or even temporary or permanent distancing when they no longer serve the common good is an act of profound care.

Starting with this chapter, the book aims to accompany each reader through this process and offer tools to broaden one's perspective, foster more honest communication, and establish boundaries that protect the emotional well-being of everyone involved, without losing the humanity that characterizes the family.

IN CLOSING

In short, the motivation to identify "false relatives" stems from a fundamental commitment to emotional truth and the health of the family fabric.

It is an invitation to observe carefully, listen intentionally, and act responsibly when the signs call for it. Ultimately, it is a commitment to bonds that sustain, enrich, and liberate, allowing family relationships to mature toward an authenticity that does not yield to convenience but is strengthened through clear boundaries, sustained empathy, and a shared sense of responsibility.

Next, we'll explore the characteristics that give false relatives away and learn to distinguish between genuine affection and disguised self-interest, using examples and practical tools to facilitate application in everyday life.

CHARACTERISTICS OF FALSE RELATIVES

Revealing behaviors emerge like a fine thread that, interwoven time and again, reveals the deep fabric of a relationship. In this chapter, we focus on those micro-signals that, when repeated over time, allow us to distinguish when someone's closeness within the family is accompanied by an interest that does not align with the well-being of the family unit.

This is not a matter of making an impulsive judgment based on a single questionable gesture; rather, it involves a careful and detailed analysis of patterns that, when observed with patience, point to a dynamic of manipulation rather than selfless care. Thus, these revealing behaviors become tools for protecting emotional health and, at the same time, for sustaining bonds that do nourish and support the family when they occur under the right conditions.

First and foremost, it is helpful to understand that these behaviors do not arise by chance. They are woven from conditional favors that appear only when there is a reward, from selective praise used to achieve a specific outcome, or from the continuous recurrence of conflicts that seem real but, deep down, are not; and there is a fundamental disagreement that serves as a pretext to intervene, dominate the conversation, or steer decisions.

A "false relative," then, may make themselves available for certain topics that grant them power or status, while remaining absent during moments requiring genuine emotional support—as if emotional intimacy had a price or a window of opportunity that they know exactly when to open and when to close.

This alternation between instrumental presence and substantive absence is one of the keys to identifying patterns; attention is focused on whatever grants control or influence, but it wanes when the issue requires vulnerability, empathetic listening, or sustained commitment without apparent benefits.

Ambiguity functions as a deliberate strategy to buy time and avoid clear commitments; whether through vague promises, plans that remain perpetually pending, or the postponement of important decisions, it creates a cushion of uncertainty that favors the person controlling the narrative.

In these cases, communication is rife with double meanings: what is said appears to be an offer of help, but in practice, it becomes a veiled condition for obtaining favors, information, or approval.

This ambiguity also makes it easier to justify contradictory behavior; mistakes are downplayed with a general apology that doesn't entail a change in habits, responsibilities are downplayed, or blame is shifted onto others to avoid personal accountability.

Here, the consistency between words and actions—an element that seems simple but is so revealing—shifts into a darker realm: people speak of support and promise to be there, but daily reality reveals planned absences or responses that only emerge when the benefit is assured.

Guilt, used as a tool, is another hallmark of these revealing behaviors. In many cases, manipulation relies on the family's emotional weight: "If you don't count on me, who's going to support you?" or "If you don't do what I say, the harmony of the household will be disrupted."

The strategy isn't simply to enforce a specific demand; it also incorporates shame or collective responsibility as an argument to get the other person to conform to a particular goal. This use of guilt can take the form of veiled reproaches, reminders of emotional debts, or insinuations that whoever refuses to give in is betraying the family.

Recognizing these tactics does not mean turning the person into an enemy; rather, it means situating the interaction within a framework of boundaries and assessing which dynamics are acceptable for the common well-being and which are attempts at control that must be confronted firmly and clearly.

Consistency between words and actions is, by its very nature, a barometer of authenticity. When someone promises to be there for you in difficult times, but their day-to-day behavior contradicts that promise—by avoiding difficult conversations, silencing criticism, or maintaining a narrative that always favors their perspective—a red flag goes up.

Added to these signs of inconsistency are cases where reciprocity in the relationship is not genuine, and while the conversation may seem balanced, emotional openness and vulnerability do not flow reciprocally. In these situations, difficult conversations become a litmus test:

Does the other person listen with empathy and respond responsibly when mistakes are confronted, or do they protect themselves and back away at any evidence of disagreement?

Careful observation of these responses provides clarity on the sustainability of the relationship. Silences also reveal a great deal, and it is not uncommon for a false relative to employ strategic silences to avoid committing or to manipulate the pace of the conversation.

Avoiding topics that might cause tension or deliberately delaying important decisions is a tactic that conserves emotional energy for opportune moments and that, at times, leaves others in a state of helplessness or constant negotiation. In this context, the question is not just "what they said" but "when they stopped speaking" and "what they left unsaid." Authentic people tend to engage fully in the dialogue; they listen, respond clearly, and maintain a genuine openness to revising agreements when reality requires it.

In contrast, strategic silences cease to be a matter of courtesy and become a form of control that hinders the building of mutual trust.

Criticism, when disguised as advice, is one of the most subtle forms of gradual demoralization. It presents itself as guidance, but its effect is to undermine confidence and sow doubt about one's own decisions.

In these cases, tone, intention, and timing make all the difference, since a comment intended to enrich or support can be productive if it is framed by respect and genuine exchange; criticism that is slipped in to point out flaws and reinforce the other person's superiority—without offering concrete help for improvement—is a sign of misaligned interests.

The distinction between well-intentioned advice and a weapon of attrition becomes clear when you ask:

Is the other person willing to take on responsibility alongside me, or do they simply want to impose their vision to gain a personal advantage?

Among the practical indicators is the way difficult conversations are handled. In an authentic interaction, people commit to understanding one another, asking questions to clarify, and seeking shared solutions, even when opinions differ. In a relationship with elements of hidden agendas, conversations often end with a sudden shift, and the other person changes the subject, avoids commitments, or reframes the discussion to make it seem as though an agreement has been reached when, in reality, there is no true compromise.

This recurring pattern is a clear warning sign that the relationship may be operating with an agenda other than that of safeguarding everyone's emotional well-being.

As an example, let's consider a hypothetical but plausible case for this analytical framework. Laura, a mother of two, notices that her cousin Diego is extremely complimentary whenever she proposes an idea that could benefit the family as a whole, but then, in private, he dismisses that same idea or suggests adjustments that would make it less viable, in favor of projects that benefit only him.

Diego offers to help organize a family trip but demands that Laura accept changes to the division of labor that favor his interests; and when Laura refuses, Diego backtracks and presents himself as the indispensable link keeping everything running smoothly, implying that "without his intervention" things would fall apart.

At meetings, Diego publicly praises Laura's generosity, but in private conversations he spreads interpretations of the discussion that portray her as unreasonable or overly rigid. In this scenario, reading the telltale signs allows Laura to distinguish between supposed support that serves only Diego's interests and a presence that could truly sustain her if they worked toward a relationship based on shared responsibility, clear boundaries, and genuine reciprocity.

Recognizing these signs is not a matter of constant surveillance or perpetual mistrust; it is a practice of discernment that seeks to protect the well-being of both partners without turning family life into an arena of constant suspicion.

Interpreting these behaviors must be accompanied by an attitude of setting boundaries—identifying where they begin and how to communicate them assertively, clearly, and respectfully.

The goal is to distinguish between genuine affection and the pursuit of self-interest, which, if left unrecognized, erodes trust and a sense of belonging over time. Ultimately, the purpose of identifying these revealing behaviors is to strengthen the bonds that sustain the family in times of crisis, without losing sight of the fact that every member deserves a safe space to express their emotions, ask for help, and move forward with emotional autonomy.

The ability to detect these signs is nurtured by continuous observation, attentive listening, and communication that prioritizes shared truth over momentary convenience.

As we move through this book, we will see how these observational tools become more precise and useful—not to label people, but to build a healthier and more sustainable framework for living together.

Interpreting these behaviors should lead, in practice, to decisions that protect everyone's well-being—with boundaries that are firmly upheld, responses that are phrased without personal attacks, and a support network that, when needed, is ready to walk alongside every family member.

In that balance between recognition and action, the possibility emerges of a way of living together that honors each person's humanity and the shared responsibility of caring for the emotional fabric that binds us together.

Revealing behaviors manifest, for the most part, as a set of subtle cues that barely catch the eye at first glance but, when analyzed patiently, reveal a structural pattern in relationships.

These are not grandiose gestures or obvious transgressions; they are repeated patterns that, over time, allow us to distinguish between a closeness that nurtures and one that exploits. At the center of these dynamics is a false relative who, even while being part of the family network or acting as such, directs their actions toward their own interests, which do not necessarily align with the well-being of the family unit.

This chapter aims to describe these revealing behaviors with precision and, above all, to provide practical guidance on how to recognize them, how to respond, and how to protect the family's emotional fabric without losing the humanity that defines it.

One of the most visible patterns of this behavior is the set of conditional favors. The act of helping appears not as an act of kindness, but as a bargaining chip that is activated only when something the other person wants or needs is obtained in return. It is common to see favors offered with an implicit reminder of debt, accompanied by a veiled demand for gratitude or future reciprocity.

This type of dynamic is not always immediately apparent, because the recipient may feel genuinely grateful and yet still find themselves trapped in a cycle of subtle dependence.

As these exchanges take place, a sort of web of unbalanced obligations is woven, which, over time, ends up forming a framework where decision-making is conditioned by the expectation of reciprocity.

Another early sign is criticism disguised as advice. Instead of a disinterested opinion, an intervention emerges that appears helpful and well-meaning but reveals an underlying interest in steering the family toward a commitment or vision that favors the speaker.

This pattern can manifest as a professional recommendation from someone who, in turn, seeks credibility or influence, or as supposedly paternal guidance that, in reality, seeks to establish leadership on certain issues. The line between genuine advice and self-serving intervention can become blurred when criticism is repeated over and over, when it is conditional on prior acceptance of certain criteria, or when constructive *feedback* is not offered but rather a framework to justify control.

The constant resurgence of conflicts where there is no real conflict is another particularly revealing micro-signal. At times, a minor issue or a minor disagreement turns into an endless cycle of dispute that only benefits the person who needs to demonstrate power or draw attention to themselves.

This phenomenon does not arise by chance; it serves as a kind of fertile ground for the "false relative" to maintain a central role—as a defender or indispensable mediator—while the rest of the family wears itself down.

When tension is repeatedly recycled, emotional energy becomes focused on disputes that lack genuine significance, resulting in an erosion of trust and a decline in the intimacy necessary for shared growth.

Selective availability occurs when a "false relative" may appear present and close only for issues that grant them power, status, or control, while systematically withdrawing when genuine emotional support or moments of vulnerability arise.

> This discrepancy between presence and empathy reveals an intention to position oneself in a comfortable place—and to be the one who receives praise or decides which topics deserve attention—without necessarily being willing to be there during difficult situations that require listening and support.

Ambiguity, as a tool for managing time and decision-making, also serves to create distance or postpone important confrontations. Vague promises, unclear commitments, and a range of responses that vary depending on the audience allow the speaker to maintain a flexibility that does not benefit the relationship as a whole.

Instead of moving toward concrete agreements, a climate of uncertainty is maintained which, in the long run, favors the person who controls the pace of the conversation. This ambiguity, in its most insidious form, becomes a barrier that prevents the family from making cohesive and responsible decisions.

Blame is often the most subtle control strategy because, by framing emotional distance or an inability to maintain closeness as a personal flaw in others, the manipulative relative manages to justify their own manipulative behavior.

Shifting the responsibility for family harmony onto others is nothing more than a sophisticated way to avoid making concessions or corrections. In these dynamics, blame does not help solve problems; it simply reinforces a silent hierarchy in which the person with the most power decides when and how to act.

Throughout these manifestations, consistency between words and actions stands as a key barometer; especially when there are discrepancies between what is said and what is done, or when promises are broken at the first opportunity for personal gain, a major red flag appears.

Genuine reciprocity—the ability to have difficult conversations without exploiting others' vulnerabilities, and the willingness to give and receive equitably—becomes a practical criterion for distinguishing between authentic affection and disguised self-interest.

Careful observation of when, with whom, and under what circumstances these behaviors emerge is essential. Not everyone who exhibits any of these traits is necessarily dishonest in every way; what matters is identifying patterns that recur in various contexts and consistently favor only one party. This article does not seek to assign blame; the goal is to help people understand that boundaries must be set so that relationships operate within a framework of respect, responsibility, and mutual care.

In that sense, the motivation for identifying these patterns is not a witch hunt, but rather a practice of strategic clarity—knowing which connections to maintain, which to reevaluate, and what decisions to make when authenticity is put to the test.

> Recognizing these signs also makes it easier to set clear boundaries and prioritize relationships that nurture over those that exploit.

The book offers tools to broaden one's perspective—such as observing consistency between what is said and what is done, distinguishing between praise that empowers and praise that manipulates, and differentiating between closeness that fosters growth and closeness that confines for one's own benefit.

This capacity for discernment is not an unyielding mistrust, but rather a pact with reality:

A family that aspires to sustain itself in complex situations needs a network of relationships marked by honesty, responsibility, and mutual support. Building on this understanding, the reader can begin to apply practical criteria in daily life.

It is not a matter of hastily labeling anyone; ideally, one should observe patiently, converse frankly, and make decisions based on what strengthens the emotional network.

This chapter, then, sets the stage for a more detailed examination of the specific characteristics of false relatives and for the techniques for assessing sincerity that will be discussed in the following sections. Ultimately, the goal is to offer a practical guide on how to distinguish between genuine affection and covert manipulation, and how to sustain relationships that, even when facing tensions, can grow in authenticity and shared responsibility.

IN CLOSING

As we conclude this exploration of revealing behaviors, it is clear that the task is neither simple nor quick, but it is necessary.

Authenticity in family relationships is not a luxury; it is a foundation for coexistence and the development of future generations.

Recognition leads to protection, and protection, in turn, unleashes the family's energy to build, day by day, a more honest and more humane environment.

This understanding—which stems from patient observation and the courageous decision to set boundaries when necessary—will serve as the foundation for the following sections, helping us distinguish more clearly between genuine affection and disguised self-interest, and offering practical tools to apply in daily life without losing sight of empathy or the dignity of each family member.

HOW TO SPOT FAKE RELATIVES

The task of assessing sincerity in family relationships requires a calm, patient, and consistent perspective. It is not about tearing down every person we live with or building castles of suspicion; what matters is discovering, with clarity and firmness, which interactions sustain the authenticity of our coexistence and which, on the contrary, manipulate or exploit closeness to gain advantages.

In this context, the techniques and strategies for assessing sincerity rely on sustained observation, on consistency between what is said and what is done, and on the quality of the responses given to difficult questions. Through this lens, each person can chart a more accurate map of their relationships, distinguish between genuine affection and disguised interests, and, based on that distinction, decide which bonds are worth nurturing and which require boundaries.

The first sign to watch for is consistency between words and actions over time. A single gesture or a well-timed comment is not enough; the key lies in consistency.

When a person promises to take an action or commits to a decision and then repeatedly fails to keep that promise, or when their stories change depending on the audience, patterns emerge that signal potential motives that do not align with the well-being of the family as a whole.

These types of inconsistencies also tend to reveal themselves in the way questions are answered—with evasive responses, excuses that are repeated in similar ways across different situations, or stories that fall apart when confronted with evidence.

In practice, carefully observing these retractions or variations can help distinguish between a closeness that nurtures and one that exploits. Consistency, therefore, is not a guarantee of goodness, but it is a solid indicator for gauging the authenticity of the relationship as a whole.

On a secondary level, the willingness to listen and admit mistakes is a crucial benchmark. A key sign of sincerity is openness to difficult conversations, the ability to listen without interrupting, and the humility to acknowledge when one is wrong or when one's account has been incomplete.

In family dynamics, resistance to admitting mistakes is often accompanied by a tendency to assign blame, shift responsibility, or portray tensions as if they were caused by others. This type of behavior reveals a form of control rather than a genuine commitment to shared well-being. Conversely, when a person demonstrates the ability to listen actively, consider different points of view, and adjust their own course when presented with new information, the foundation of the relationship is strengthened, and space is created for fairer, more collaborative resolutions.

The presence of genuine reciprocity in conversations—that is, an exchange in which both parties share, support, and accompany one another—further reinforces the sense that the relationship is based on principles of mutual respect and responsibility.

The third dimension that allows us to distinguish between genuine affection and disguised self-interest is genuine reciprocity. It is not enough to offer support in times of crisis; that support must be sustained, and there must be a balance between giving and receiving over time. In this regard, the quality of the conversation plays an important role:

- Are emotions and decisions shared with a similar level of openness?
- Is there an intention to understand the other person beyond immediate convenience?
- Are conversations about sensitive topics handled with care and without attempting to take advantage of the other person's vulnerability?

These observations allow us to assess whether interactions strengthen the relationship or, on the contrary, tend to turn closeness into a space of one-sided influence.

In families, authenticity is sustained when decisions are made with a holistic perspective, with respect for everyone's needs and a willingness to support one another without expecting hidden benefits.

The fourth dimension relates to testing boundaries and the ability to say no, to create distance when necessary, and to demand clear conditions—which is not a sign of mistrust, but rather of relational maturity.

In the presence of a genuine bond, the other person will understand that these boundaries are necessary for the emotional health of the family network and will agree to negotiate in good faith. Conversely, when the assertion of boundaries is perceived as a threat or when the other person responds with pressure, blame, or manipulation to force a response, this indicates a less balanced relationship that is more prone to exploitation.

Setting boundaries protects the integrity of interactions, fostering an environment where each person can express their needs without fear of retaliation or loss of status.

To practice these techniques, it is helpful to develop a set of practical tools that facilitate observation and conversation. Keeping a record of relevant interactions can help identify recurring patterns over time—such as what is offered, what is requested, how conflicts are addressed, what happens when the other person listens, and what the dynamics are when tensions arise. Direct questions, phrased clearly and without judgment, allow one to probe intentions and boundaries without provoking excessive defensiveness; consistent and humble responses typically indicate authenticity, while shifting or evasive responses often signal a greater need for vigilance.

Assertive communication—based on expressing needs firmly but without personal attacks—facilitates clearer dialogue and reduces the likelihood of misunderstandings that fuel manipulation.

In short, utilize tools such as constant observation, record-keeping, clear questioning, and assertive communication to maintain a framework where truth is verified by facts rather than insinuations.

Patience and practice are indispensable allies; and recognizing signs of sincerity is not a one-time act, but rather a process that is refined over time, through experience, and through the responsibility of caring for the family network.

This path requires taking a realistic look at the dynamics that sometimes present themselves subtly—such as kind gestures that hide ulterior motives, compliments seeking personal recognition, or displays of closeness that are maintained only under certain circumstances.

The ability to distinguish between these variations improves when one cultivates a broad perspective while also paying close attention to the details of each interaction. In this way, people can decide with greater clarity which relationships deserve priority, which require less flexible boundaries, and which spaces can remain open for mutual growth. In this context, the goal is neither to treat every family member as a suspect nor to dismantle the emotional network at the first sign of interest.

The goal is, on the one hand, to protect the family's emotional well-being and, on the other, to strengthen bonds that truly nurture and sustain. When the signs of sincerity are accurately recognized, it prevents giving in to unjustified pressure, minimizes the erosion of trust, and fosters a climate of cooperation that allows disagreements to be addressed with dignity.

This approach, which begins with observation and is grounded in open conversation and respect for boundaries, sets the stage for the following sections, which will expand the repertoire with practical examples and specific tools for assessing sincerity and distinguishing between genuine affection and disguised self-interest.

The final reflection on these techniques invites us to understand that the ability to assess sincerity in family relationships is not an end in itself; it is a means to foster a more humane and responsible coexistence. When people learn to discern between what nurtures and what exploits, the family emerges as a space for mutual growth and emotional security.

This does not mean shielding oneself from the possibility of conflict; ideally, one should learn to manage tensions with clarity and a continuous commitment to truth and shared responsibility.

Within this framework, every interaction becomes an opportunity to strengthen trust, foster empathy, and, at the same time, protect the dignity of everyone involved.

If this approach is maintained, family dynamics can evolve into a more authentic network—one that is less susceptible to manipulation and better able to support future generations in an environment of mutual respect and support.

The distinction between true and false relatives is not achieved through isolated intuition; it is achieved through a set of practical tools that allow us to read the dynamics beneath the surface of family relationships.

This chapter aims to describe, clearly and without sensationalism, the tools for distinguishing between genuine affection and disguised self-interest, and to do so, it draws on two fundamental pillars: the observation of patterns and the quality of communication.

These tools are linked to the book's central ideas of protecting the emotional health of the family network, strengthening authentic bonds, and intelligently navigating the tensions that can arise when closeness intersects with manipulation.

The aim is not to demonize anyone or turn the family into a laboratory of mistrust; rather, the goal is to equip each reader with practical criteria to decide—based on repeatable facts and honest conversation—where it is worth investing energy and where it is advisable to set boundaries.

First and foremost, observing recurring patterns serves as the cornerstone of this book. A false relative often operates through subtle cues that, taken together, reveal an underlying objective and their own utility or influence within the family network.

Among these signs are conditional favors, in which help is provided only if reciprocity that benefits the other person is satisfied; praise that appears selectively to gain favors or to reinforce a narrative that benefits that person; and recurring conflicts where, at first glance, there would be no real conflict, or an escalation of tensions that seems to divert attention from truly relevant issues.

These signs should not be interpreted in isolation; they must be analyzed as pieces of a mosaic that, when observed in different contexts, reveal a pattern of subtle influence seeking to control decisions, resources, or relationships. Interpreting these patterns requires patience and a willingness to distinguish between what nurtures and what exploits.

Repetition is no coincidence; it is a sign that there is a mechanism driving the actions, and that mechanism can be understood and managed if it is clearly grasped. Alongside pattern recognition, active listening emerges as an essential complement to interpreting the situation.

Listening is not limited to hearing words; it involves grasping intentions, unexpressed tensions, and possible inconsistencies between what is said and what is done. Active listening is put to the test when addressing sensitive or conflict-ridden topics; by paraphrasing what has been heard and asking open-ended questions, you can determine whether the person is willing to confront issues honestly or tends to deflect, justify, or blame others when tensions arise.

Genuine reciprocity is a crucial sign: when someone shares and offers support in the same tone and with the same openness both with you and in the presence of others, the relationship tends to be sustained by a genuine balance.

On the other hand, if the person offers support or comments only in certain contexts, or if they avoid difficult conversations, this is a red flag. Active listening also involves observing how the other person handles emotional topics:

- Do they admit mistakes and correct their account when inconsistencies are pointed out?
- Do they avoid blaming others and take responsibility when appropriate?

These responses provide a more accurate assessment than any superficial analysis. Clarity of communication, for its part, is the third pillar. Assertive communication—which expresses needs, boundaries, and expectations without personal attacks—makes it easier to distinguish between genuine affection and self-serving interest. When a person communicates clearly, there is consistency between what they say and what they do over time, and it is evident that they use language that avoids ambiguity to buy time or manipulate others.

Expressing boundaries directly and respectfully is a practice that, beyond defining the limits, sends a signal that relationships are governed by clear rules. Asking for clarification when inconsistencies arise and validating one's own perceptions with concrete examples helps prevent misinterpretations and sustain a productive dialogue.

In cases of tension, assertive communication does not seek to win an argument, but rather to open pathways to a genuine resolution and a shared understanding of what each person needs and expects.

Keeping a record of interactions is a practical, everyday tool. This record is not a chronicle of paranoid monitoring; rather, it serves as a map of observable behaviors—what is offered, what is requested, what happens when there is conflict, and how the other person responds when listening.

A log allows you to see patterns over time and detect subtle changes that aren't apparent in a single conversation; this method also helps clarify your own memory in the face of belated or biased accounts.

The combination of observation, listening, and recording forms a tripod that guides decisions; that is, if the relationship is grounded in these three pillars, authenticity is strengthened; if any one of them fails, prudence suggests reassessing the intensity of the bond. The application of these tools relies on simple, everyday exercises. For example, when important decisions arise, it is helpful to ask direct questions about intentions and boundaries: "What do you expect from my support on this issue?" or "How could I help you without creating an unreasonable expectation for you?"

The answers should be examined carefully, looking for consistency between words and actions, and assessing whether the person is willing to adjust their behavior when necessary.

Humility in the face of mistakes and a willingness to change are valuable indicators of authenticity, while a tendency to blame others or shift responsibility are red flags. These criteria, applied with patience, allow us to distinguish between relationships that strengthen us and those that seek to exploit a situation for personal gain.

A particularly valuable practical aspect is evaluating support during difficult times; authentic people demonstrate their presence during crises, maintaining trust and avoiding complicity that benefits only one party.

Conversely, when support appears to be conditioned by self-interest or is reduced to superficial gestures without a foundation of continuity, it is reasonable to reconsider the importance of that relationship within the family network.

This assessment should not lead to an automatic conclusion that all closeness is dangerous; the goal is to understand what kind of support is offered, when, and with what consistency, in order to decide whether the relationship should be maintained as a source of support or whether it is better to distance oneself to protect everyone's emotional well-being.

The tools described here are not rigid formulas or tests for immediately labeling someone; they are lenses for perceiving more precisely what nurtures and what undermines mutual care.

The practice of observation, frank conversation, and keeping a brief record of interactions become habits that strengthen each member and the quality of the family's emotional fabric.

This emphasis on strategic clarity does not seek to sow mistrust; rather, it aims to provide a framework that allows each person to make informed and responsible decisions, especially when faced with complex dynamics that, if left unaddressed, tend to erode existing trust and harmony.

In terms of everyday application, these tools should be integrated into a relational style that prioritizes honesty, respect, and mutual care, because the goal is not to reject the family or turn family life into a barren landscape; rather, it is to build bonds that sustain and nurture, even when conversation requires firm boundaries or when it is necessary to seek outside support to manage tensions.

The tools described here allow those who practice them to navigate ambiguous situations with greater confidence, to distinguish between affection that strengthens and favors that exploit, and, above all, to sustain a network of bonds that, over time, proves to be more authentic and resilient.

IN CLOSING

To wrap up, it's important to remember that these tools shouldn't be viewed in isolation; they should be integrated into a deeper layer of emotional awareness—that is, personal intuition, fueled by experiences, healthy boundaries, and a commitment to the family's well-being.

Intuition, when grounded in observable evidence and clear communication, becomes a powerful guide for navigating the line between closeness that nurtures and closeness that manipulates.

Ultimately, this set of tools aims to provide the reader with a perspective that protects the emotional fabric without sacrificing the humanity of relationships. When practiced regularly, observation, active listening, and assertive communication transform daily interactions into a laboratory for more authentic coexistence, where differences can coexist with respect, and where family love has the strength necessary to endure over time.

REAL-LIFE CASES OF "FALSE RELATIVES"

This chapter delves into stories and examples that, far from being mere anecdotes, serve as mirrors reflecting the dynamics of false relatives in the daily lives of families. The goal is not to assign blame in each story, but rather to carefully observe the signs that, over time, reveal a set of interests that do not always align with the well-being of the family network.

In these narratives, closeness does not guarantee honesty; proximity can be used as a setting for carefully calibrated praise, conditional favors, or gestures of support that, deep down, seek to gain influence, power, or resources. Based on these experiences, it is possible to identify patterns that, when repeated in different contexts, allow each family member to distinguish between genuine affection and manipulative strategies.

The common thread is to look beyond appearances, listen to what is left unsaid, and protect the integrity of one's close-knit network, even when the emotional cost is high.

One of the most common narratives involves a family member who, in public, offers kind words while engaging in veiled scheming behind the scenes. An aunt or cousin who presents themselves as unconditional support, celebrating every achievement in front of everyone, yet suggests or makes immediate help conditional on certain demands.

In these stories, reciprocity is not equitable; rather, their constant presence serves to secure favors or to restore the speaker's image. However, the amount of resources given or expected to be received is unbalanced.

The lesson that emerges from this pattern is the need to distinguish between support that nurtures and support that, in reality, demands an emotional debt. When a gesture of closeness comes with hidden conditions, it is reasonable to ask who is gaining and at what cost to others.

This type of narrative invites us to observe whether the promise of support holds up in complex situations or, on the contrary, fades in the face of decisions that demand shared responsibility.

Another recurring narrative centers on the figure of the advisor who offers criticism disguised as advice. In this narrative, a close acquaintance insists on setting criteria or passing judgment on every family dilemma, presenting their opinions as a necessary guide to protect the common good.

Behind that facade of helpfulness, there is often an agenda that favors the speaker; constant criticism can function as a tool of control, a subtle way to divert attention from their own mistakes or their particular interests.

Over time, these interventions create an atmosphere in which important decisions are delayed, distorted, or postponed to avoid confronting a reality that might challenge perceived authority.

In these stories, the true test lies in the consistency between words and actions; for when criticism is accompanied by a willingness to correct one's own positions, the gesture takes on a sense of authenticity; when, however, criticism remains a constant without reciprocal accountability, an instrumental dynamic is revealed.

A third narrative useful for understanding the phenomenon describes emotional manipulation through guilt; in these situations, a person within the inner circle uses guilt as a lever to influence decisions or to dismiss the responses of others.

The mechanism is subtle because it leads people to believe that distancing themselves or questioning certain behaviors is equivalent to betraying a family member, when what is at stake is each person's freedom to set boundaries and look after their own well-being.

This type of narrative highlights the difference between shared responsibility and exerting pressure to maintain a *status quo* that benefits the person imposing the rules.

The lesson is clear: guilt must not become a common tool for negotiating behavior or silencing legitimate criticism; each person's emotional autonomy must be respected, even when the cost is distancing oneself from an influence that no longer nurtures.

There is also a category of stories that depict the cultivation of discreet alliances to preserve or expand family influence.

In these stories, certain bonds are strengthened by their ability to bring in allies, gain visibility, or consolidate a lineage of power.

The agreements that take shape often present a facade of harmony, but they are based on a web of favors and promises that depend on the presence of—or the risk of losing—advantages.

In these narratives, criticism of rivals is often presented as concern for the common good, when, in practice, the goal is to build a support network that sustains the position of the person coordinating these agreements.

The lesson that emerges is the need to monitor the dynamics of influence and to ask whether the consistency between what is said and what is done holds up when the context changes or when the temptations to gain benefits increase.

No single story, on its own, is sufficient to identify the presence of false allies; however, taken together, they point to a set of warning signs worth keeping in mind.

Conditional favors that leave a constant debt, praise that becomes a bargaining chip, criticism that sounds helpful but actually directs attention toward a particular version of reality, and a willingness to help that appears selective when it comes to issues that benefit the speaker.

These are the micro-signs that, when repeated in different scenarios, allow anyone to turn suspicion into a more precise and less emotional observation.

> The key lies in the practices of reading the affective network: noting what is offered and what is requested, observing what happens when there is conflict, and analyzing how the other person responds when listened to without interruptions or preconceived judgments.

This careful observation becomes a tool for clarity, helping us decide which relationships to continue investing in and with which it is wiser to reduce our involvement.

Reading these stories is not intended to label everyone who expresses affection as a potential manipulator. On the contrary, it invites us to distinguish between the form of expressing support and the substance of the action.

When closeness remains stable despite the need to set boundaries, when reciprocity is expressed through gestures and words that stand the test of time, and when decisions are made with shared responsibility and an openness to correcting mistakes, the authenticity of that relationship is confirmed.

Conversely, when closeness is used to reinforce a position of control, when promises become unfulfilled norms, and when guilt functions as a means of pressure to obtain favors, the reader can recognize that they are facing a dynamic that, sooner or later, erodes and distorts the family experience.

By presenting these stories and their lessons, this chapter aims to equip the reader with a more discerning eye for interpreting close relationships. The goal is not to demonize anyone; rather, it is to build a framework for understanding that allows us to distinguish between genuine affection and disguised self-interest.

This distinction is essential for protecting the family's emotional cohesion and for learning to set boundaries when necessary, without losing the humanity that characterizes family relationships.

The stories gathered here lay the groundwork for the following sections, which will explore specific characteristics of false relatives and techniques for assessing sincerity that facilitate decision-making in everyday life.

By understanding the sources of tension, each reader will be able to identify, with greater clarity and composure, which bonds are nurturing and which—no matter how close they may seem—require a reassessment of their place within the emotional network.

Reading real-life cases in this section of the book reveals, more clearly than any abstract theory, the decisions people make when the pressure to maintain an image of family harmony clashes with the reality of hidden agendas.

In these narratives, closeness does not guarantee honesty; there are those who promise support, grant favors, or offer discreet praise while pursuing goals that, deep down, benefit one party rather than the whole.

This pattern does not seek to demonize anyone, but rather to expose a reality that is sometimes hidden behind pleasant conversation, warm visits, and kind words. Understanding these dynamics requires a careful reading of what lies between the lines—such as what is said, what is avoided, how people react to certain topics, and what is concealed when the topic becomes a source of power or influence.

When analyzing these stories, decisions emerge that determine outcomes and either safeguard or erode the emotional health of the family network.

One of the most visible decisions is giving in to pressure to maintain apparent harmony; in these situations, the person chooses not to confront the issue, to downplay or even silence uncomfortable truths in order to avoid confrontations that could trigger a larger conflict.

This type of choice, motivated by the desire to avoid immediate pain, often takes a cumulative toll, as the truth is postponed, tensions build up, and, over time, the disconnect between what is said and what is done becomes more apparent.

In the best-case scenario, an atmosphere of tolerance is momentarily achieved, but at the cost of requiring greater effort to maintain that facade when new tensions arise.

Another common approach is to prioritize family loyalty over the truth, especially when making decisions involving resources or reputation. In these circumstances, the family becomes entangled in a narrative that promotes outward cohesion, presenting a unity that appears solid to outsiders but conceals internal divisions.

The dichotomy between upholding the shared narrative and embracing the truth can generate guilt and confusion; for guilt, far from being a mere feeling, sometimes functions as a tool of control and is used to justify one-sided confidences or to delegitimize doubts that challenge the dominant narrative.

This path can sow resentment among those who perceive that reality is being sacrificed to maintain an image of unity, and among those who understand that honesty is the foundation of lasting bonds.

Finally, there are decisions aimed at severing ties to protect one's own well-being, because when the emotional cost of maintaining a relationship with a supposed relative becomes too high—due to constant manipulation, emotional blackmail, or a sustained erosion of trust—the way out may be to distance oneself.

This is a defensive move that, while it may bring immediate relief, also involves mourning the loss of a figure who, due to their shared history, alternated between closeness and coldness, between occasional support and manipulative pressure.

The process of distancing oneself is not cruel by default; rather, it is strategic and seeks to preserve one's own integrity and that of those around us, especially when the harm seems to repeat itself or multiply over time.

In these cases, clarity often comes too late for some people —when toxic dynamics have already been allowed to take root or when the memory of broken promises weighs heavily on the mood of future gatherings.

These decisions do not occur in a vacuum; they are accompanied by a constellation of signs that, when observed with patience, allow us to anticipate outcomes and decide with greater serenity where to invest our energy and set boundaries.

Reading these stories teaches us that authenticity is not mere window dressing; it is a prerequisite for sustaining relationships that nourish us, even in the midst of tensions. When a relationship is grounded in truth, that truth sets boundaries that allow the bond to remain a space for mutual growth and shared responsibility.

Conversely, when the weight of self-serving motives takes hold, conversations lose their honesty, and family life can deteriorate with every decision that prioritizes a particular benefit over the common good.

A key lesson that emerges from these reflections is that authenticity is a sustainable necessity in family life, not a luxury.

Decisions that protect the integrity of the emotional fabric—even if they involve saying no, distancing oneself, or rethinking agreements—tend to hold up better in the face of the stresses of time.

Relationships that age with dignity are those in which clarity of intent is accompanied by consistent actions, the ability to apologize when appropriate, and the willingness to adjust behavior when evidence suggests that something isn't working.

In this sense, maintaining a prudent distance can become a strategy for care, not a punishment, and the respectful confrontation of differences can be an act of responsibility that strengthens trust in the long term.

Reading these cases also highlights a central aspect of family life, specifically the need to distinguish between genuine affection and utilitarianism. Sometimes, gestures of closeness are presented as recognition and support, but they conceal a calculation of benefits that does not align with everyone's well-being.

Recognizing these signs requires a constant practice of observation, listening, and dialogue, without falling into constant suspicion or indiscriminate distrust.

The goal is to develop practical criteria that allow us to interpret reality honestly and without resorting to simplistic judgments. Although this may sound demanding, tools are provided to sustain healthy bonds and prevent the tensions of family life from becoming a burden that prevents future generations from experiencing relationships based on trust and respect.

In this chapter, the review of decisions and consequences is presented as a practical foundation for the subsequent stages of the book. The aim is for the reader to internalize the idea that bonds are strengthened by a network of consistent behaviors, shared responsibility, and clear boundaries—not by mere physical presence or the promise of support.

Authenticity thus emerges as a skill cultivated through daily interaction—by listening intentionally, demanding clarity when there is ambiguity, expressing needs without attacking others, and, above all, maintaining the willingness to adjust course when the evidence calls for it.

It is this capacity for insight, gentle assessment, and responsible action that will enable us, in the following pages, to address more effectively the specific characteristics of false relatives and the practical techniques for assessing sincerity, setting boundaries, and protecting the family's emotional well-being without sacrificing the empathy and care that define a genuine family.

IN CLOSING

All in all, the conclusion of this section points to a fundamental idea: family life requires a commitment to the truth that overcomes the temptation to bend reality to fit a convenient narrative.

The integrity of family bonds is sustained when each member is able to discern, amid the complexity of relationships, what fosters growth and what causes strain.

If reading these stories awakens in each of us the awareness that certain patterns must be confronted and managed with human limits, then the purpose of this chapter will have been fulfilled.

This is not about stigmatizing anyone; the ideal is to protect a network of relationships that deserves to be nurtured with courage, patience, and a clarity that allows us, day by day, to build a family that is more authentic, more just, and better able to sustain its members over time.

Based on these considerations, this chapter invites readers to the next stage: understanding in detail the specific characteristics of false relatives and learning to distinguish between genuine affection and disguised self-interest through tools for assessing sincerity, communication practices, and well-defined boundaries.

Through careful reading, open dialogue, and responsible decisions, it is possible to strengthen trust and protect the family's emotional well-being, even when external tensions threaten to tear it apart.

This is the path toward bonds that, despite trials, are sustained by honesty and enriched by the shared responsibility of caring for future generations.

THE IMPORTANCE OF TRUST AND INTUITION

Intuition is neither an isolated gift nor a mystical flash of insight; it is the result of constant practice in mindfulness and observation of the dynamics that shape family relationships. Understanding, in practical terms, how to develop and trust intuition allows us to turn that insight into a guide for more conscious and responsible decisions, which strengthen the emotional bond rather than erode it.

Intuition, understood in this way, emerges when the mind remains present in the moment, when initial impressions are noted and tested through direct and respectful conversation. It does not seek to replace evidence; rather, it guides it and is nourished by repeated experiences, by the consistency between what is said and what is done, and by the ability to admit mistakes and adjust course when reality contradicts a first impression.

To cultivate this kind of intuition, it is helpful to start with presence—that is, to pause in the middle of an interaction, take a deep breath, and try to notice what sensations arise without rushing to interpret them.

In practice, this means noting—even briefly—the signals you perceive: a tone of voice that becomes sharper, a smile that doesn't match the subsequent action, a silence that settles in when sensitive topics arise.

These cues, observed repeatedly over time, begin to weave an internal map that makes it easier to distinguish between closeness that nurtures and closeness that exploits. On this map, intuition is not a definitive judgment; rather, it serves as a signal indicating the need to investigate with greater clarity and honesty.

A second key aspect is testing initial impressions through simple questions and open conversations. This does not imply blind distrust; rather, it is a way to confirm or refute hypotheses that arise from observation.

For example, when a concern arises about assistance offered "on behalf of the family," a direct question can be asked about the actual scope of that assistance, the associated conditions, or the potential benefits for the other person.

The way the question is answered, the consistency between what is said and what is done, and the speed with which errors are corrected or misunderstandings are clarified often provide valuable insights. The intention is not to confront; the idea is to shed light on the reality behind the words. It is also helpful to distinguish between emotional intuition and rational assessment.

Emotion can point to sensitive areas, such as a sense of suspicion, discomfort, or unease that recurs every time you interact with a certain person. Rational assessment, on the other hand, examines concrete facts such as consistency between words and actions, consistency over time, the quality of reciprocity, and the ease or difficulty of having difficult conversations without taking advantage of others' vulnerability.

The combination of both perspectives, when practiced honestly, usually leads to more confident decisions and an emotional framework that protects the family without falling into paralyzing cynicism.

Active listening plays a central role in strengthening intuition.

Listening with intention involves putting ourselves in the other person's shoes, but without losing the ability to listen to our own experience. It means allowing the other person to explain their motivations, even when they are uncomfortable, while remaining attentive to signs indicating a discrepancy between what is said and what is done.

Practicing active listening also involves asking questions that clarify boundaries and expectations.

For example, when someone proposes an agreement or arrangement, asking about timelines, responsibilities, and potential emotional costs helps dispel the fantasy of selfless cooperation and brings us closer to the reality of the relationship.

Intuition develops and strengthens through accumulated experience in diverse family contexts.

It is not about collecting isolated events as if they were conclusive evidence; rather, one must observe recurring trends and patterns—such as which topics tend to trigger controlling behavior, what gestures accompany broken promises, and when a person is present versus when they disappear without explanation during moments of vulnerability.

This interpretation, carried out with patience, gradually transforms into a framework of emotional security that allows each member to decide with greater clarity where to invest their energy and set boundaries.

It is a process that requires humility and the recognition that intuition can fail, that the first reading won't always be accurate, and that the truth may require several layers of conversation and review. One practical way to strengthen your intuition is to create a "signal map." This map is not a rigid list of rules; it is a flexible guide that highlights which behaviors are typically associated with self-interest and which tend to reflect genuine support.

Keeping a brief record of relevant interactions helps identify patterns over time. For example, recognizing that certain favors come with demands or that criticism always arises in the same context can help put an initial intuition into perspective. This map should go hand in hand with the practice of setting clear boundaries and the ability to create distance when necessary, so that intuition does not become an excuse to avoid emotional commitment; rather, it serves as a tool for maintaining healthy and responsible relationships. In everyday practice, intuition is also nourished by an ethic of care, because the decision to act with honesty and foster a climate of trust does not imply constant mistrust, but rather a willingness to engage in dialogue with empathy and clarity.

When intuition points to possible manipulation, the appropriate response is not a hasty accusation; ideally, it would be to initiate a structured dialogue to express specific concerns, ask for verifiable examples, and propose conditions for sustaining the relationship.

This approach strengthens trust because it demonstrates a commitment to truth and respect for each person's emotional autonomy within the family.

Imagine a sister who offers financial support for a specific need but always makes the help conditional on accepting certain decisions she proposes for the benefit of her own circle of influence. Upon observing this pattern, intuition might indicate the need to clarify the conditions and assess the actual reciprocity.

Instead of reacting with anger, you can initiate a focused conversation and ask what exactly she intends with that support, what will happen if circumstances change, and what other resources exist to address the need without relying on that help.

The answers and the consistency of her actions in the following weeks will be the key test for deciding whether it's worth maintaining the relationship with firm boundaries or whether it's better to distance yourself to protect everyone's emotional well-being.

This type of practical exercise strengthens intuition and the ability to act responsibly in times of stress.

Trust in intuition, to be useful, must coexist with an ethic of shared responsibility. It is not about turning intuition into a sole authority that replaces reasoning; rather, it is about making it a complement that guides decisions toward relationships that sustain, respect, and nurture.

Over time, this way of interpreting family dynamics fosters a more mature way of living together because it recognizes the authenticity of affection, distinguishes between gestures that seek power and those that seek care, and builds a framework in which truth, empathy, and clear boundaries allow the family to grow without losing the humanity that defines it.

Ultimately, intuition becomes an ally that facilitates daily discernment, from casual conversation to the most significant decisions that sustain the well-being of the emotional network.

In short, developing and trusting intuition is a form of human growth closely linked to clarity, patient observation, and the willingness to converse honestly.

It is a practice that deepens as mindfulness, the ability to read subtle cues, and shared responsibility grow stronger.

This approach sets the stage for the upcoming sections of the book, which will explore strategies for strengthening trust in genuine relationships and turning intuition into a practical tool for building healthier bonds, safeguarding emotional well-being, and educating future generations in a model of coexistence based on truth, respect, and compassion.

> Trust in genuine relationships is an ongoing process that is nourished by clarity, consistency, and the ability to remain steadfast in the face of the tensions inherent in any family life.

In this chapter, we aim to provide practical tools to strengthen that fabric that allows us to feel security, belonging, and autonomy all at once.

Trust is not built on pretty promises alone; it is grounded in the repeated experience that words and actions align, in the openness to express what hurts or worries us without fear of judgment, and in the willingness to support one another even when the truth requires confronting differences.

This framework draws on intuition when integrated with reasoned assessment, because, as we will see, intuition is best honed when there is empirical evidence of consistent behavior over time.

One of the keys to strengthening trust is cultivating open communication free from premature judgments; this involves creating spaces where each participant can express fears, hopes, and disagreements without fear of being dismissed or reduced to a stereotype.

Openness does not mean laying all one's weaknesses bare at once; rather, it means practicing active listening and listening to understand, not to prepare a defensive response. In practice, this translates into questions that invite clarification and responses that seek to rebuild bridges rather than shut down conversations. When people feel that their experiences are taken seriously and that words match actions, trust is solidified as a shared resource—not through the absence of conflict, but through the responsible management of differences.

Recognizing clear boundaries is another fundamental pillar, because trust matures when every family member knows which topics require special care and which can be discussed more freely.

This recognition is not a rigid wall; it is a framework that protects everyone's dignity and prevents tensions from becoming tainted by accumulated resentments. Communicating boundaries clearly, empathetically, and specifically prevents misunderstandings and reduces the likelihood that ambiguous behaviors will be interpreted as gestures of support.

When boundaries are established, honest conversation is facilitated, and people no longer have to guess whether an action is a gesture of closeness or a veiled condition. Much of the strength of family bonds lies in that balance between sincerity and courtesy. Constructive sincerity is another powerful tool because it's not about turning every conversation into a thorough examination of blame; rather, it's about expressing needs and concerns based on one's own feelings and on observable facts.

Practicing constructive honesty means avoiding sweeping criticisms and focusing on specific behaviors—such as what was said, what was expected, and what the outcome was. This approach reduces the emotional burden that often accompanies criticism and fosters cooperation in finding practical solutions. When people sense that the intention is to support—not to hurt or gain an advantage—the conversation can become fertile ground for agreements that benefit the family network as a whole.

True reciprocity, for its part, is a barometer of authenticity in relationships. It implies that support and the willingness to listen and offer guidance do not depend on a single gesture or a favorable circumstance; ideally, they are consistently present over time and in different contexts.

This principle does not require perfect equality in every interaction, but it does require an emotional balance sufficient to ensure that no one feels used or invisible.

Celebrating progress, no matter how small, strengthens this dynamic of cooperation and fosters the motivation to continue investing time and effort responsibly. In the long run, the network is sustained by the trust that emerges when acts of care are repeated and become predictable.

The diversity of support sources is another essential ingredient for sustainable trust. When people rely on a broad and trustworthy network—friends, mentors, professionals, other family members who demonstrate integrity—they do not depend on a single relationship for their emotional balance. This diversity reduces vulnerability to potential tensions in a specific relationship and broadens the avenues for personal and collective growth. It is not about turning everyone into confidants; the goal is to build a network of trust that provides support in times of crisis, change, or doubt.

It is in this sense that the family learns to value the intimacy of close bonds and the strength provided by a set of relationships that share principles of honesty, responsibility, and mutual support.

Managing conflicts through direct dialogue, without resorting to destructive confrontation, is a practice that strengthens trust.

Differences are inevitable; what matters most is how they are addressed. Structured opportunities for conversation are recommended, where each person can express their version of events, supported by concrete examples, and where listening prioritizes understanding over winning an argument.

This approach prevents conflicts from turning into power struggles that wear down the emotional bond and erode trust.

At the same time, the ability to apologize and correct mistakes in light of the evidence from the experience creates a climate of security that encourages continued investment in the relationship.

Humility and personal responsibility are qualities that strengthen trust in a sustainable way. Recognizing one's own mistakes, admitting when one has failed, and making concrete commitments to correct course is essential.

This kind of attitude—rather than making excuses or justifying actions—provides people with a foundation of trust because they know that, even when they make mistakes, they are seeking the common good and not personal gain.

Shared responsibility, moreover, becomes a pillar of cohesion, and when each member takes on their share of the responsibility for resolving a situation, the entire network is strengthened, and the likelihood that a relationship will become unbalanced due to isolated failures is significantly reduced.

To illustrate these ideas, let's consider a practical, realistic scenario that might arise in a family experiencing tensions over expectations of emotional support during a period of change. Imagine Ana and Carlos, a couple with two teenage children, who notice that their older sister, Luisa, is almost always present when it suits her, but absent when they need support during times of vulnerability or grief.

Luisa offers praise and advice when there is social pressure or when the family needs to maintain an image of unity, but her availability dwindles when the issue is emotionally difficult or when ongoing support is needed.

Ana and Carlos then decide to establish a routine of weekly dialogue with Luisa and other close family members during a 45-minute meeting where everyone expresses concerns and sets boundaries, followed by a written summary of agreements and responsibilities.

They also agree to diversify their support network, seeking connections with other family members and friends who demonstrate consistency in their behavior and a willingness to provide support in various circumstances. Over time, Luisa learns that her presence must be sustained during times of pain, not just when it serves to uphold an image of harmony.

The experience allows the family to see that trust is not a promise or a label; it is the result of sustained actions rooted in consistency, empathy, and shared responsibility.

IN CLOSING

The final reflection that emerges from these guidelines is simple yet powerful: trust in genuine relationships cannot be improvised—it must be cultivated.

It requires an attitude of gentle vigilance, in which we observe patterns without losing sight of the humanity that characterizes each bond. It is about cultivating a balance between the openness that fosters intimacy and the boundaries that protect emotional well-being. It is, at the same time, a call to humility—to accept that no one is perfect, but that we can choose to support those who demonstrate consistency between what they say and what they do.

In this way, the emotional network is strengthened and expanded with reliable, supportive individuals, and the family, as a system, adapts to grow with confidence in the face of life's inevitable stresses.

This approach sets the stage for the next sections of the book, in which we will delve into specific tools for distinguishing between genuine affection and hidden agendas, as well as strategies for maintaining healthy bonds without losing the humanity that gives meaning to family life.

STRATEGIES FOR DEALING WITH FAKE RELATIVES

Limiting the impact of false relatives requires a deliberate strategy that combines clear boundaries, assertive communication, and mindful management of the spaces where family relationships unfold. It is not about closing doors or turning the family into a cold fortress; rather, the ideal is to weave an emotional network in which authenticity and mutual care are sustained even in the face of pressures or behaviors that seek to exploit closeness.

Within this framework, the first step is to identify which issues are non-negotiable for the well-being of the family unit and which, by their nature, can be addressed with greater composure or under different circumstances. Defining these boundaries is not an act of harshness; rather, it is a way to protect the trust that allows relationships to function over time.

When it is clearly established what is acceptable and what is not, a framework is created that reduces ambiguity and facilitates consistent responses to attempts at manipulation.

Defining clear boundaries is a central component of the strategy, and this involves making a precise distinction between what can be discussed cordially and what requires a firm and protective stance.

For example, some issues may require a direct, brief conversation focused on verifiable facts, while others should be addressed in more controlled settings or even outside the immediate circle if discussing them would be harmful to the group's emotional well-being.

In this regard, consistency between words and actions becomes a key sign of integrity. Promises that cannot be kept or that are offered solely as a bargaining chip to gain benefits must be identified and dismissed as a basis for trust.

Maintaining consistency between what is said and what is done strengthens the credibility of those who operate within boundaries, and that credibility ultimately serves as a buffer against future tensions.

Assertiveness emerges as the practical tool for upholding these boundaries. Expressing needs, boundaries, and expectations directly yet respectfully—without personal attacks—helps the other person understand which behaviors are acceptable and which are not. This approach avoids fruitless back-and-forth and reduces the energy spent on unnecessary arguments.

Furthermore, assertiveness entails a sense of responsibility because when a conflict arises, it is preferable to point out the observable behavior that is causing distress and propose concrete alternatives, rather than accusing the other person of having ulterior motives.

To the extent that difficult conversations are approached with a sense of shared responsibility and the intention to strengthen the family network, the dialogue can move toward effective solutions without damaging the relationship.

Managing spaces for interaction is another key element, because limiting exposure to certain dynamics in large gatherings, setting specific times for contact, and prioritizing written communication for sensitive topics are practices that reduce the likelihood that manipulation will unfold in a public setting and worsen the situation.

Large family gatherings, when not necessary to resolve urgent matters, can become settings for social pressure and the pursuit of approval from others.

In such cases, structuring meetings with a clear framework, defined time limits, and basic rules for participation helps keep the conversation on a constructive track and prevents old tensions from resurfacing in a disproportionate way.

Consistency between words and actions is reinforced by responding simply and firmly to attempts at manipulation. When someone tries to evade commitments, make vague promises, or resort to blame to justify problematic behavior, the response should be brief, concrete, and fact-based—focusing on what is expected, what has been agreed upon, and the next step. Avoiding prolonged debates that fuel conflict is a practical skill that, over time, becomes a habit;

clarity reduces the likelihood of misunderstandings and minimizes the emotional strain that accompanies underlying tensions.

> Simply put, the more direct the conversation, the easier it will be to maintain boundaries without turning every interaction into a confrontation.

Not underestimating the need for outside support is another essential aspect. In many circumstances, effectively setting boundaries requires resources and perspectives that go beyond what the family can provide internally.

Family mediation or professional counseling can provide tools to revitalize the conversation, establish fairer agreements, and, when necessary, facilitate healthy distancing without recriminations.

This external support does not undermine the humanity of the relationship; it protects it by fostering an environment where differences can be expressed with dignity and where decisions are made with a balanced perspective.

A practical framework for applying these ideas emerges when boundaries, assertiveness, space management, and external support are combined into a coherent plan. The plan should not be viewed as a rigid checklist; rather, it should be presented as a set of principles that guide day-to-day decisions regarding which issues are priorities, how to say "no" without causing hurt, and when to seek support to sustain the emotional support network.

In practice, this can translate into actions such as establishing a communication protocol for sensitive issues, agreeing with the family on a meeting schedule that prevents the recurrence of conflicts, and arranging for a neutral third party to facilitate difficult conversations.

The central aim is to uphold each person's dignity while, at the same time, protecting the integrity of the family as a whole.

To illustrate these ideas, let's consider a case study that, in the absence of a shared real-life situation, may represent a plausible experience for many readers. Imagine a family preparing for an annual gathering and facing pressure from an aunt who insists that all her children receive a certain amount of financial assistance for a personal project.

The initial conversation takes place in a cordial tone, but quickly becomes uncomfortable when the aunt suggests that, if her demand is not met, the family unit could face discord among siblings and criticism from the community.

At this point, the family decides to activate its boundary protocol: they clearly specify what kind of support is possible and under what circumstances such assistance would not be feasible; they agree not to discuss this issue in large gatherings and, instead, move the conversation to a smaller session with a mediator if necessary.

They choose to communicate the conditions and deadlines in writing, so that there is no room for misinterpretation. With this framework in place, the family can maintain harmony at the external gathering without yielding to the pressure of the request, while preserving everyone's relationships and emotional well-being.

This example illustrates that limiting the impact does not mean isolating oneself; it means designing responses that are consistent, fair, and oriented toward the common well-being, even in the face of attempts at manipulation.

The invitation is to understand that the effectiveness of these strategies depends on consistency and shared responsibility. Limiting the harm that false relatives can cause is not a tactic of constant confrontation; it is a practice of care that seeks to balance need and dignity. By setting clear boundaries, maintaining consistency between words and actions, and seeking outside support when appropriate, the family not only protects its present well-being but also strengthens the foundation for future generations.

In the following sections, we will explore more specific tools for assessing sincerity and reinforcing boundaries with practical examples, always aimed at sustaining genuine bonds without losing the humanity that characterizes family life.

The goal is clear: to build a more mature family dynamic, where the intention to care is not overshadowed by manipulative control, and where each member can contribute responsibly to the well-being of the whole.

Setting clear boundaries is one of the most practical strategies for reducing the influence of false relatives without losing the humanity that characterizes family life.

It is not about erecting insurmountable walls; what matters is establishing protective boundaries that allow affection and responsibility to coexist, without one party taking advantage of their closeness to gain benefits at the expense of the common good.

Within this framework, techniques for setting boundaries are based on three fundamental pillars: assertiveness, clarity in expectations, and consistency in responses. Each of these components provides a key element that enables the family network to withstand tensions while continuing to cultivate genuine bonds.

Assertiveness:

This involves the discipline of expressing one's needs without losing respect for the other person or undermining the dignity of the relationship.

It involves expressing boundaries directly, without personal attacks or accusations that fuel conflict. In practice, this means focusing the conversation on observable behaviors and the effects of those behaviors on oneself and on the family, rather than burdening the conversation with ambiguous interpretations or judgments about the other person's intentions.

For example, when faced with repeated pressure from a family member to provide financial assistance or to influence family decisions, an assertive response could be articulated in a brief and clear statement: "I cannot provide that assistance at this time; if the situation changes, we will discuss it at another time and with specific limits." This clarity prevents arguments from escalating and focuses on what is acceptable and what is not.

Clarity on expectations:

This involves making it clear, in specific terms, what is expected from each relationship and what behaviors are consistent with mutual care.

It is crucial to distinguish between forms of support that strengthen autonomy and those that stem from an unequal exchange. Expectations must be realistic and verifiable; they should specify, for example, what kind of emotional support is offered, under what circumstances help can be sought, which gestures or favors should be reciprocal, and which should not become conditions for interaction.

This clarity prevents misunderstandings that erode trust and makes it easier for each party to understand what is at stake when disagreements arise. In practice, this can take the form of simple agreements, such as defining in advance which issues are non-negotiable and which can be discussed with some flexibility, without compromising one's integrity.

Consistency in Responses:

This is the most challenging aspect of complex family dynamics, as consistency between what is said and what is done creates a framework of predictability that reduces anxiety and strengthens trust.

When a person promises something today and fails to follow through tomorrow without a reasonable justification, the ability to uphold boundaries is undermined. Consistency does not imply rigidity; it means that, even when boundaries are adjusted in light of new circumstances, those changes are communicated transparently and are based on clear criteria.

Maintaining consistency also requires documenting agreements when necessary, as a written note of what was agreed upon can serve to remind parties of their commitments and prevent differing interpretations as time goes on.

In this sense, consistency between words and actions becomes a compass that guides the relationship toward a place of greater trust and genuine reciprocity.

A central part of the proposal is the distinction between non-negotiable issues and those open to discussion. Non-negotiable issues are typically linked to personal dignity, the emotional security of the most vulnerable members, and the integrity of the family unit. These issues require firm boundaries and clear responses when they are threatened.

On the other hand, there are issues that can be discussed with room for negotiation and under reasonable conditions, always within a framework that does not compromise the family's well-being or expose anyone to abusive or manipulative situations.

The balance between these two types of issues is dynamic and should be reviewed regularly, especially when new situations arise or changes occur in the family structure. This periodic review helps adjust boundaries without losing the humanity of relationships, preserving a sense of belonging and shared responsibility.

> The practice of saying "no" with empathy is another key skill. Saying "no" is not an act of rejection but of care, because it protects both the person expressing it and the person receiving it, while maintaining the possibility of developing alternative solutions that sustain the relationship.

Instead of a blunt refusal, an empathetic response offers a supportive approach: acknowledging the other person's need, explaining why the current request is not feasible, and proposing an alternative that allows the relationship to remain intact without sacrificing one's own well-being.

Empathy, in this context, does not mean giving in to pressure; rather, it means seeking solutions that respect all parties and maintain the relationship on a collaborative footing.

Developing a strategy for gracefully exiting unavoidable situations is another practical tool. Sometimes, even with clear boundaries, an interaction may arise that significantly disrupts one's emotional balance.

In such circumstances, having a well-articulated exit strategy—a respectful and gradual way of parting ways that minimizes harm—can prevent abrupt breakups and facilitate the distancing that may be necessary for the sake of emotional well-being.

This script is not intended to demonize the other person or deny the shared history; it seeks to bring a phase of the relationship to a close in the most humane and responsible way possible, leaving open the possibility of a future reunion under healthier conditions.

Documenting agreements and reviewing them periodically is not a bureaucratic hurdle; it serves as a practical tool for maintaining boundaries over time. Writing down what was agreed upon, in what context, and under what review criteria ensures that boundaries do not depend on the selective memory of each moment.

This practice facilitates the objective observation of progress and, when necessary, adjustments—whether to relax a rule or to tighten it in light of new risk dynamics. Periodic reviews should be conducted with the participation of those directly involved and, when appropriate, with the support of mediation or professional counseling to ensure that decisions continue to prioritize the common well-being.

The management of spaces and interaction formats also plays a practical role. In large meetings, for example, it may be appropriate to limit the discussion of certain topics or to standardize the way sensitive issues are addressed.

Establishing defined contact schedules and favoring written communication for sensitive topics can reduce the likelihood of escalations and misunderstandings. This readjustment of interaction environments is not a restriction on the relationship; rather, it is a design that protects everyone and facilitates daily coexistence, even when tensions rise.

A diverse range of support systems and a support network also strengthen the enforcement of boundaries. When people turn to different sources of support—friends, mentors, therapists, other family members—the emotional burden does not fall disproportionately on a single relationship.

This diversity reduces dependence on a single source of support, which could otherwise become a lever for manipulation. In practice, cultivating a broad and reliable support network is an act of care that complements the protective barrier of boundaries and promotes the emotional autonomy of each member.

IN CLOSING

In closing, it is important to remember that the influence of false relatives is not combated with harshness; it can be addressed with a combination of clarity, consistency, and humane solutions. Boundaries must be upheld firmly, yet with enough flexibility to adapt to circumstances without sacrificing the dignity or warmth of the relationship. This balance may require practice, patience, and, at times, outside support.

With these tools, the family can continue to grow in harmony, even when facing inevitable tensions, strengthening trust, shared responsibility, and the ability to care for one another without sacrificing their own well-being.

The central idea that emerges from this set of strategies is that boundaries are a framework that facilitates sustainable coexistence, not a rigid barrier that cuts off the relationship.

Clarity in expectations, assertiveness in communication, and consistency in responses form a three-pronged foundation that supports each member's emotional autonomy while keeping open the possibility of respectful, meaningful human connections.

As these practices are incorporated into daily life, the family network is strengthened, the pressure of veiled manipulation is reduced, and space is created for the emotional fabric to grow with greater freedom and responsibility.

Chapter by chapter, the book guides readers in transforming well-defined boundaries into a more authentic and secure sense of belonging for present and future generations.

CLEARING OUT TOXIC RELATIONSHIPS

Clearing out toxic relationships is a gradual process that stems from an honest assessment of the impact of each relationship on one's own well-being and that of the family network. At this point in the book, the aim is not to offer a definitive diagnosis or a condemnatory judgment, but rather a careful examination of the reality each person experiences at home.

Identifying which dynamics drain you, which behaviors repeat themselves, and which emotional responses frequently arise is the first step toward clearly deciding where adjustments should be made and, if necessary, creating some distance. This assessment, which may seem harsh, is actually an act of self-care and responsibility toward those with whom you share daily life, because a family is not strengthened by keeping the truth at bay; it is strengthened by aligning actions with mutual care that sustains everyone in the long term.

To move forward firmly in this direction, it's helpful to narrow our focus, since no one denies that affection can coexist with tensions and wounds; the key lies in distinguishing between bonds that nourish and those that repeatedly exploit closeness for their own benefit.

In practice, this distinction becomes clear when we assess the emotional cost of certain interactions, and questions that may previously have gone unnoticed become necessary:

- What patterns recur when the relationship is at stake?
- What emotional responses are most frequently triggered in the presence of that person?
- What happens when there is conflict or when difficult decisions must be made that affect the family as a whole?

Answering these questions honestly allows us to construct an internal map of boundaries and courses of action that protect emotional well-being without losing the humanity that characterizes a healthy family life.

A key part of this chapter is the recognition that creating distance is not the same as punishing or rejecting someone. Creating distance, when necessary, is an act of care—a way to preserve the emotional balance of everyone involved and to prevent the chronic strain of a relationship from poisoning the overall atmosphere of the home. This approach does, however, require planning that respects both the other person's dignity and one's own.

It is not about cutting ties entirely; the ideal is to reduce, reorganize, and, in certain cases, reconfigure the way you interact. The intention is clear: to accelerate the recovery of emotional energy, make room for nurturing bonds, and consolidate an environment in which shared responsibility and mutual respect can emerge more strongly.

Within this framework, reducing contact should be viewed as a concrete strategy, not as an impulsive emotional reaction. Start by decreasing the frequency of interactions that have been particularly draining or that have shown patterns of exploitation.

This initial step can reveal the true weight of the relationship and facilitate decision-making. It is also helpful to communicate the changes clearly and calmly, explaining the reasons without unnecessary embellishments or excessive justifications.

Transparency prevents misunderstandings and avoids burdening the other person with unnecessary guilt. The goal of this first step is to preserve as much dignity as possible for both parties, keeping the lines of communication open for courteous treatment and, if appropriate, for controlled interaction when the context allows it.

If the situation does not improve, it may become necessary to distance oneself in a more planned manner. This distancing should be gradual, with minimal communication, and focused solely on the well-being of everyone involved.

Even during this process, the goal is not to fuel a conflict; rather, the aim is to protect emotional well-being. In practice, this may mean opting for less frequent meetings, limiting the person's involvement in sensitive matters, or delegating certain decisions to other family members who offer greater stability.

At the same time, it is advisable to strengthen an external and alternative support network—such as trusted friends, mentors, or professionals—who can provide solid emotional support capable of sustaining personal autonomy when the family of origin does not consistently offer that support.

Experience shows that the period of distancing can be painful, and it is common to feel guilt, fear of severing meaningful bonds, and anxiety that the decision will be misinterpreted by others.

> It is essential to remember that self-care is not a whim, but a prerequisite for the family to sustain itself in the medium and long term amid inevitable tensions.

Clarity of purpose—preserving emotional health, protecting future generations, and maintaining the ability to build authentic bonds—helps sustain the decision when emotions run high. Furthermore, consistency between words and actions serves as an anchor; if you say you're going to reduce contact, it's essential that your actions match that commitment to prevent the distance from being perceived as permanent absence or rejection.

In the context of this chapter, it is worth presenting a case that illustrates the process without stylizing it in a moralizing way. Let's imagine a family living with an aunt who, although close to them, tends to pressure them for favors and use guilt to reinforce her influence.

At first, the family tries to maintain harmony through gestures of tolerance and promises of support, but recurring dynamics reveal significant emotional strain caused by arguments arising from issues that should be neutral, unfulfilled promises that leave others with the burden of maintaining balance, and a tendency to form alliances based on veiled criticism aimed at others' weaknesses.

After an honest assessment, the family decides to reduce the frequency of gatherings, establish clear boundaries regarding topics to be discussed, and adopt a more structured format for interaction.

In specific cases, they may agree to hold meetings in broader settings with other family members present, or even include a mediator to keep the conversation within a framework of respect and responsibility.

Over time, the planned distance becomes more stable, and the family finds the energy to nurture bonds that truly strengthen relationships—such as the relationship between siblings and the bonds between parents and their teenage children—which require mindful presence and a climate of trust that cannot depend on a single person.

This example underscores a central idea: distancing is not used to assign blame or demonize; it is done to restore the possibility of coexistence that, at its best, is grounded in honesty, shared responsibility, and mutual care. In practice, this also means seeking outside support when necessary.

The help of a mental health professional, or participation in mediation sessions, can facilitate the process, especially when the family faces difficult dilemmas or when attempts at dialogue become tense and repetitive.

The ultimate goal is to maintain a balance that allows each person to exercise their emotional autonomy without losing the human connection that gives meaning to family life.

The invitation is to understand that clearing out toxic relationships is not so much a protocol as it is a constant mindset. It involves anticipating tensions, distinguishing between genuine affection and manipulation, and making responsible decisions about when to maintain, adjust, or distance oneself. It is a commitment to a future in which future generations learn to recognize signs of manipulation, to express their needs clearly, and to sustain bonds based on truth, empathy, and shared responsibility.

That is why setting boundaries can be a decisive step in protecting the fabric of the family, without losing hope that—through healthy boundaries and a diverse support network—it is possible to cultivate relationships that nurture, educate, and strengthen everyone who is part of the family's story.

Self-care and emotional protection are not whims; they are necessary conditions for sustaining human bonds amid family tensions and distances that sometimes become unavoidable.

In the process of clearing out toxic relationships—where one learns to identify draining dynamics and to distance oneself responsibly—self-care becomes a survival skill that allows one to maintain serenity, even when close coexistence has become difficult.

This self-care does not seek to isolate the individual; rather, it focuses on preserving the ability to love with clarity, to show empathy without constantly exposing one's vulnerabilities, and to uphold emotional responsibility without allowing toxic bonds to dictate the course of family life.

Understanding self-care as the foundation of healthy relationships involves redefining the concept of well-being, since it is not a static state of perpetual happiness but rather an ongoing practice that sustains the tension between intimacy and boundaries.

When the family goes through periods of discord, when power dynamics or manipulation resurface in certain gatherings or conversations, taking care of oneself becomes an ethical act. It means recognizing what one can receive without neglecting what one needs to give in order to preserve personal dignity and the integrity of the group. This approach distinguishes between the effort to maintain a bond and the sacrifice of one's own emotional well-being. In this balance, self-care emerges as a support system that protects not only the individual but also the family network as a whole.

To cultivate this system, it is helpful to incorporate specific habits that strengthen emotional resilience. One of the pillars is regular reflection—setting aside time to review what has happened, identify which emotions arise in each interaction, and distinguish between impulsive reactions and thoughtful responses.

Reflection is not self-punishment; it is a calm examination of recurring patterns, and pairing it with sufficient rest is another crucial element. Emotional exhaustion depletes one's capacity for discernment and makes it easy to confuse the need for closeness with the desire to avoid conflict.

Getting enough sleep and taking a break from lengthy meetings or biased accounts that may circulate within the family are simple actions that preserve clarity and strengthen the ability to respond with restraint.

Seeking professional support when necessary is a legitimate and prudent part of self-care. Talking to a therapist or family counselor provides an external, neutral space to clarify perceptions, practice assertive responses, and develop conflict-management strategies. The goal is not to diagnose or blame anyone; what matters is gaining the tools to maintain emotional well-being in the face of complex situations.

This support can facilitate the development of action plans, such as agreements for temporary separation, safer communication routines, or techniques to defuse emotional escalations.

Seeking professional help also involves emotional economics—recognizing when it makes sense to invest in outside guidance that brings structure to your relationship.

Among the specific practices that strengthen self-care, personal rituals stand out as a way to maintain mental clarity and presence in daily life. A ritual can be as simple as setting aside a moment in the morning for mindful breathing, taking a short walk to release tension, or taking a brief break during the day to write down three things you're grateful for.

These habits are not forms of escapism; they are anchors that help maintain a perception of reality as it is, without allowing toxic dynamics to take on disproportionate importance.

Cultivating friendships and trusting relationships outside the immediate family circle also acts as a healthy counterbalance; these are people who offer consistent emotional support, listen without judgment, and reinforce each individual's positive contribution to the family fabric.

Emotional protection, for its part, is exercised with clear boundaries and a practical understanding of what one is willing to tolerate. Protecting one's well-being involves deciding, with clarity, which issues should be addressed under certain conditions, what degree of closeness is sustainable, and what is the appropriate forum for certain conflicts.

It's not about cutting off all communication; rather, it's about adjusting it so that emotional energy is used constructively.

A boundary might be, for example, limiting exposure in situations where each person's personal space is threatened by derogatory comments, or establishing rules about which topics are addressed in which contexts.

Maintaining consistency between what is said and what is done is crucial so that words do not become mere empty promises and so that actions support the intentions of mutual care.

Another aspect of self-care is building a diverse support network, because relying on a single source of emotional support can become a vulnerability; if that source were to fail, the family's balance could be thrown off.

Therefore, it is helpful to cultivate relationships with friends, mentors, professionals, and other family members who share values of honesty and responsibility.

This diversity does not imply generalized mistrust; rather, it provides additional security, because in the face of tensions or crises, there are human and material resources that support the process of distancing oneself with dignity and without guilt. In practice, a broad network makes it easier to benefit from different perspectives, reduces the burden on any one individual, and keeps the focus on solutions that benefit the family as a whole.

Implementing these practices has a direct impact on the ability to make difficult decisions, such as easing tensions or temporarily separating from certain relationships.

When self-care is consistently practiced, difficult decisions lose some of their emotional weight and become strategic actions aimed at well-being.

In this context, distancing oneself is a protective measure designed to preserve people's ability to love, collaborate, and grow within a framework of respect and responsibility; it should not be confused with an act of punishment.

This approach promotes a more mature way of living together; while it does not deny the humanity of relationships, it protects each person's dignity and prevents the pressure of toxic dynamics from clouding family life.

Throughout this chapter, it is emphasized that self-care also involves recognizing when the path of least harm is to seek external support and reconfigure the network of relationships that sustain the family.

The idea is not to isolate oneself to avoid contact; rather, one should create an environment where each individual can manage their emotional life autonomously, without sacrificing a sense of belonging or the possibility of rebuilding bridges when circumstances allow. In this sense, self-care becomes an investment in one's own mental health and in the emotional well-being of others, because when a person nurtures their own inner peace, they, by extension, convey that peace to the group as a whole.

As we look to the future, this topic of self-care and emotional protection ties in with the practical tools that will be discussed in the following sections.

We will explore methods for distinguishing more precisely between genuine affection and hidden agendas, and propose strategies for maintaining healthy relationships without losing the humanity that underpins family life.

For now, the essential thing is to recognize that clearing out toxic relationships is not a sacrifice of one's own joy; it is a discipline that facilitates a more authentic life and a home capable of sustaining all its members through adversity and joy.

In this vein, consistent self-care serves as the driving force that enables us, day after day, to courageously choose between compassionate engagement and the necessary defense of our own emotional well-being.

IN CLOSING

A final reflection on the importance of self-care and emotional protection invites us to consider three central ideas.

- First, clear boundaries and consistency between what is said and what is done are expressions of respect both for oneself and for others.
- Second, diversifying one's support network strengthens emotional autonomy and reduces dependence on a single source of validation.
- Third, the consistent practice of self-care habits—rest, reflection, mindfulness, and, when needed, professional support—transforms necessary distancing into a responsible decision and, at the same time, an affirmation that humanity and dignity can remain intact even in the face of family tensions.

On this foundation, the family can move toward a more mindful way of living together, in which each member learns to take care of themselves so they can better care for others.

CONSEQUENCES OF FAILING TO IDENTIFY "FALSE RELATIVES"

When not detected in time, false relatives can set off a cascade of consequences that affects the entire family network and the emotional climate of each individual. Ignoring warning signs is not simply overlooking clues; it is allowing self-serving dynamics to take root as the norm, gradually eroding the trust, clarity, and emotional security that sustain the family as a whole.

In this chapter, we explore the risks and harm that arise when emotional vigilance weakens and the authenticity of relationships is left at the mercy of hidden agendas. We thus aim to understand why it is important to respond with calm and foresight to patterns that, if allowed to grow, turn everyday life into a slippery slope.

The first consequence is the repetition of conflicts that, rather than being resolved, become routine; for when a dynamic is governed by disguised interests, disagreements cease to be about specific issues and instead become tools for exerting pressure, buying time, or reinforcing a position of power within the family.

Thus, conversations that should clarify boundaries, decisions, and emotions veer off into endless arguments, where the truth becomes blurred amid conflicting accounts, half-truths, and broken promises. This constant mistrust fosters an atmosphere in which every interaction carries the weight of an unspoken suspicion:

Is what is being said enough
to sustain the relationship, or is there a hidden agenda
that conditions everything?

Over time, this uncertainty breeds exhaustion and unease, and the hope for harmonious coexistence is undermined by the feeling of walking on unstable ground.

Another dimension of the damage is the erosion of trust—not only among those directly involved, but also in the family's collective memory.

When actions do not match words, and when favors or praise are used as bargaining chips to secure personal advantages, the shared history loses its integrity. The stories told at gatherings, the promises that are repeated, and the support offered with strings attached are all marked by a persistent suspicion.This erosion of trust is not an isolated failure; it is a wound that is passed down through generations. Younger family members, upon realizing that there is no consistent alignment between what is said and what is done, internalize a dangerous lesson: that truth and affection may be subject to the convenience of the group or an individual, rather than serving as stable foundations for coexistence.

Chronic stress is a third consequence that often accompanies these dynamics. The constant need to scrutinize intentions, question gestures, and anticipate possible maneuvers generates sustained emotional tension.

Far from promoting greater prudence, this state tends to undermine the mental and physical health of those exposed to the instrumentalization of relationships. Chronic stress also impairs the ability to make clear-headed decisions, since when the mind is preoccupied with watching for possible deception, the clarity needed to distinguish what is genuine from what is manipulative is diminished.

This means that people may end up prioritizing the emotional numbness of superficial coexistence, rather than cultivating bonds that nourish and strengthen the family in the long term.

The repercussions extend beyond the present and into future generations. When dynamics of affection and self-interest become normalized as a pattern of family interaction, children and adolescents learn to measure their worth based on the approval or favor of someone in a position of relative power within the family. This lesson can sow insecurities, a fear of expressing disagreement, and difficulty distinguishing between genuine love and disguised manipulation.

The emotional upbringing of new generations risks becoming a lesson in excessive caution, in which asking for help or expressing a need is interpreted as a sign of weakness or as an opportunity to be taken advantage of. The harm, therefore, is not only personal; it is social and generational.

Given this scenario, recognizing the risks early on makes a crucial difference. Early detection allows each family member to act with greater composure, build a more balanced environment, and prevent dysfunctional patterns from taking deep root.

Careful observation of family dynamics, combined with a practical approach to boundaries, honesty, and shared responsibility, can prevent a seemingly close relationship from becoming an instrumental one.

The goal is not to turn family life into a realm of total mistrust, but rather to clarify what is expected of each relationship and how that relationship either supports or undermines the common well-being.

Within this framework, the book offers a path to addressing these risks without blaming anyone or demonizing complex family relationships. First, it is helpful to map out recurring behaviors that signal hidden agendas, such as conditional favors, selective praise, criticism disguised as advice, complicit silence in the face of inappropriate behavior, and an unbalanced emotional investment.

This mapping is a strategic interpretive tool that helps distinguish between genuine affection and manipulation.

Second, it is essential to cultivate open communication and active listening, which allow us to differentiate between genuine concern and an attempt at manipulation. Speaking clearly, setting boundaries, and asking for clarification when inconsistencies arise are practices that strengthen the family network and reduce vulnerability to power dynamics.

Readers' experiences, however diverse they may be, can be framed within simple and plausible examples that illustrate these principles.

Let's imagine a family that, when faced with a controversial issue, follows the same pattern: either the conversation yields a useful outcome for everyone, or it turns into a power play for one individual.

On one occasion, a close relative offers their "support" in exchange for avoiding questions about certain decisions affecting shared resources. On another, public praise is accompanied by veiled criticism in private that seeks to undermine the autonomy of those on the sidelines.

These examples are not meant to point fingers; however, they help illustrate patterns that, if repeated, must be identified and addressed with clear boundaries and honest communication.

As we conclude this section, it's worth remembering that preventing harm requires a combination of vigilance, boundaries, and external support when necessary. Recognizing that a close relationship can also be a source of emotional strain requires courage and humility to take action.

The goal is to protect the emotional well-being of the entire family and to preserve the possibility of building more authentic bonds in the future.

In the following sections, specific tools will be developed to distinguish between genuine affection and disguised self-interest, as well as strategies for addressing these dynamics in a practical and humane way.

Maintaining the humanity of family life, even in the face of tensions, is a commitment that requires careful discernment, responsible decision-making, and a supportive framework that allows each member to grow with dignity and clarity.

Avoiding manipulation or deception is not a matter of constant mistrust; rather, it involves building a way of living together that promotes truth, clarity, and shared responsibility.

When a family faces dynamics in which hidden agendas lie behind gestures of closeness, the risk is real, trust erodes, decisions become ambiguous, and harmony seems to be maintained only at the expense of a truth that is set aside.

In this scenario, prevention is just as important as response; the goal is to create tools that enable people to detect warning signs, verify facts, and maintain an environment where they can trust one another without losing their autonomy or emotional stability.

This chapter proposes a set of practices that, together, aim to strengthen that foundation by documenting verifiable facts, engaging neutral observers, and fostering transparent communication that debunks narratives convenient for one party while, at the same time, protecting others.

Let's start with the need to document verifiable facts, because documenting does not mean turning every interaction into legal evidence; rather, it means preserving a clear and objective record of what happened—such as dates, topics discussed, promises made, commitments undertaken, and results delivered.

This record serves as a counterbalance to narratives that, over time, can become selective or distorted.

When someone close to you offers praise or does you a favor, it's natural to feel grateful; however, memory tends to become biased under emotional pressure, and that's where keeping an operational record becomes crucial.

Writing down what was agreed upon, checking whether those promises were kept, and noting any shifts in position regarding the topics discussed helps separate emotion from the facts necessary for decision-making.

It's not about turning every interaction into a formal record; it's about creating an accessible log that allows you to compare what was promised with what was actually done, and to detect patterns that indicate sustained manipulation or the exploitation of closeness to gain an advantage.

The second key element is consulting neutral third parties. In this context, the idea is not to delegate the responsibility for discernment to an outsider to resolve the situation, but rather to obtain a perspective that is not biased by the family tensions of the moment. A family therapist, a mediator, or even a trusted friend who has no direct involvement in the conflict can offer a different framework for interpreting behaviors that, in the privacy of the family, might seem confusing or justifiable.

The key is to choose people who listen without prejudice and who are willing to question narratives clouded by emotion.

This external support does not replace each family member's responsibility; however, it adds a layer of clarity that makes it easier to distinguish between genuine support and manipulation disguised as help.

> Questioning narratives that benefit only one side is another fundamental principle.

In the context of family relationships, we often encounter narratives that absolve the benefactor of responsibility and that, paradoxically, seek to legitimize their own position under the guise of family loyalty. Questioning does not mean becoming a relentless judge; it means applying a critical eye to explanations that readily align with a particular version of the story. Direct, well-formulated questions can pave the way for understanding real intentions and effects.

- What purpose underlies that action?
- What benefit, if any, is sustained in the long term?
- What evidence supports that version of events?

This process of inquiry, applied with empathy and without accusation, helps prevent a biased narrative from overshadowing the shared truth and ensures that cooperation does not become a tool of control.

Transparency in communication is another pillar, and when conversations are open and candid, intentions are more likely to be laid bare, reducing the likelihood of misunderstandings that fuel suspicion.

Transparency means clarifying the intentions and boundaries of each interaction; for example, when dealing with a sensitive issue, it can be helpful to clearly state what is expected, what is considered acceptable, and how compliance will be verified.

Clarity of intentions makes it easier for everyone involved to understand the context of the conversation and prevents a genuine act of support from being mistaken for a ploy to gain influence or control.

Emotional education within the family serves as a long-term tool for sustaining these practices; it involves teaching every member—from the youngest to the adults—to identify warning signs without turning them into disproportionate fears.

At the same time, it involves discussing emotions, boundaries, and responsibilities—and doing so in a way that makes each person feel heard and validated.

Emotional education is not a task isolated from therapy or parenting; it is a habit cultivated through regular conversations, rules of respect, and simple exercises in recognizing internal states.

When people learn to express concerns without aggression and to ask for clarification when doubts arise, the emotional support network gains resilience and the ability to withstand stress.

Mental health, as a whole, must be integrated into the strategy through practices such as mindfulness, emotional regulation, and, when necessary, consultation with professionals—all of which help maintain personal balance while navigating complex dynamics.

This is not a luxury; good mental health is the foundation that enables each person to distinguish between legitimate pressure and covert manipulation, and to retain the ability to make decisions with clarity and responsibility.

A shared approach to mental health within the family, including mutual support, can transform a potentially hostile environment into a space where everyone's dignity is protected and harm is prevented from spreading to future generations.

A culture of shared responsibility, for its part, is the framework that brings these practices together into a cohesive whole.

It means accepting that each member plays an active role in the common well-being, that the truth must be sought and accepted by all, and that decisions must be made with the interests of the network as a whole in mind, not just those of one party.

In practice, this translates into explicit agreements, periodic review of commitments, and a calm vigilance toward signs of imbalance.

When responsibility is shared, the temptation to exploit others loses ground to the conviction that the family's prosperity depends on the integrity of its relationships.

Ultimately, the integrity of family relationships rests on consistency between words and actions, on the willingness to seek the common truth even when it is uncomfortable, and on each person's ability to take on a share of the responsibility in the face of tensions.

This set of practices does not guarantee that conflicts will not arise or that all disputes will be resolved without pain; what it does offer is a clearer path for distinguishing between affection that nurtures and self-interest that exploits, and for deciding with greater serenity when it is reasonable to maintain a relationship and when the best option is to temporarily distance oneself—in a spirit of care rather than punishment.

Ultimately, the goal is to strengthen bonds that support everyone's emotional well-being, protecting future generations and fostering a way of living together marked by authenticity, responsibility, and shared empathy.

IN CLOSING

The final reflection invites us to view these practices as an operational framework for documenting facts, consulting neutral third parties, questioning biased narratives, and fostering open and clear communication.

With this framework, the family can navigate more confidently through situations where individual interests may diverge from the common good, without constant suspicion becoming an obstacle to harmonious coexistence.

If each person embraces the truth responsibly and commits to the collective well-being, the dynamics of control and sabotage find less ground to thrive, and the emotional network is strengthened to withstand tensions and changes.

This approach, applied consistently, lays the groundwork for the strategies discussed in the following chapters, which address concrete tools for assessing sincerity and establishing boundaries that protect the family without losing the humanity that gives it meaning.

HOW TO PROTECT FUTURE GENERATIONS

Protecting future generations begins with instilling solid values, including honesty as a constant guide, empathy as a bridge across differences, responsibility as a shared commitment, and the establishment of healthy boundaries that support each member's emotional autonomy.

This foundation of education and values does not arise from a single moment; it flourishes through daily practice that becomes woven into the rhythm of family life. It involves cultivating an environment in which words and actions, from childhood onward, demonstrate consistency: promises are kept, criticism is rooted in a desire to help, and what is valued remains free from the competition for favoritism.

This consistency lays the foundation for future generations to learn new concepts and develop a way of being that enables them to discern, act, and care for others without losing their inner freedom.

Emotional education is one of the central tools in this chapter. Educating in the realm of emotions involves teaching young people to identify what they feel, to name it clearly, and to express those feelings without fear of judgment.

That first step opens the door to a candid dialogue about the expectations placed on them, social pressures, and potential manipulation that may be disguised as care or concern for their well-being.

When children and adolescents learn to talk accurately about their emotions, they acquire a common language for discussing boundaries, disagreements, and aspirations.

This process does not eliminate conflict, but it transforms it into a constructive conversation that helps them understand what truly benefits them and what might be exploiting their affection or trust.

Within this framework, the family takes on an active role in teaching children to question external expectations. The goal is not to discourage legitimate ambition or stifle young people's natural curiosity, but rather to teach them to distinguish between an aspiration that fosters their development and pressure that seeks to mold them for the benefit of others.

By cultivating an attitude of gentle questioning, we help the younger generations avoid accepting anything by default, because every norm, every tradition, and every form of affection must be justifiable in and of itself—especially when the balance between family closeness and personal autonomy is at stake. An education grounded in values strengthens the ability to say "no" clearly when appropriate, without feeling guilty, and to ask for help when a sign of manipulation or imbalance is detected.

Responsibility, in its practical sense, translates into concrete habits that can anchor family life by fulfilling commitments, accepting the consequences of one's own actions, and participating in the creation of fair agreements that take all members into account.

> Responsibility is not a straitjacket; it is a framework that allows each person, from childhood onward, to understand how their actions impact the collective well-being.

When young people see adults owning up to mistakes, correcting their course, and allowing for open discussion, they learn to do the same in their own relationships—that is, with friends, at school, and in the community.

This transfer of habits is, in itself, a valuable legacy that prepares future generations to navigate complex dynamics without losing their ethical sense of coexistence.

Family traditions can be powerful allies when cultivated with transparency and fairness. The customs, celebrations, and stories that have been passed down from generation to generation must not become mechanisms of exclusion or privilege, because they are elements that strengthen shared identity without shielding anyone from internal or external criticism.

The key lies in making the meaning of these traditions explicit, in reassessing their relevance in light of new realities, and in inviting all members to contribute their voices to enrich them.

When traditions are lived out with clarity, they become spaces for learning and for strengthening bonds based on respect and truth, rather than inherited burdens that hinder the emotional development of new generations.

Teaching healthy boundaries emerges as an essential component of this chapter. It is not about contradicting affection or discouraging closeness; on the contrary, it is about protecting each individual so they can love and be loved without losing their personal dignity.

Setting boundaries explicitly, using simple phrases and concrete examples, helps young people appreciate that relationships require clear conditions to be sustained.

Learning to negotiate boundaries with empathy and to adapt them as circumstances change is a practical skill that prepares young people for adulthood, where responsibilities and stresses become more complex.

The central idea is that boundaries do not close the heart or block communication; boundaries, when properly understood, facilitate a more authentic and secure coexistence, in which trust can grow on a more solid foundation.

Values education also involves developing the skills to ask for help and to recognize when it is necessary to seek support outside the family. Teaching children and adolescents to identify available resources—trusted friends, teachers, counselors, mental health professionals—strengthens their emotional autonomy and their ability to cope with difficult situations.

The idea is that the family should not be the only refuge; it should serve as a core that accompanies and facilitates the building of a broad and reliable support network. By learning to turn to others when appropriate, future generations learn to share the responsibility for their well-being and to avoid excessive dependence on a single source.

In practice, values education takes shape through regular conversations, moments of active listening, and simple empathy exercises. For example, a weekly conversation in which each member shares an achievement and a concern, followed by a shared reflection on how everyone's words and actions contribute to the group's well-being, can become a ritual that reinforces what has been learned.

Within this framework, it is essential to teach people to ask questions respectfully, to express concerns without fear of reprisal, and to acknowledge when someone has made a mistake—apologizing and proposing solutions. Such practices, repeated consistently, create an environment where people feel valued, secure, and committed to the common good.

A hypothetical scenario can help illustrate these ideas without relying on the experiences of others. Let's imagine a family that is building a new dynamic of coexistence in which a close relative offers gifts or favors in exchange for influencing decisions regarding schooling and child-rearing.

Instead of silently accepting this, the parents call a family meeting, explaining that while they do not question the relative's affection, agreements regarding education and boundaries must be discussed and agreed upon by all responsible adults.

They establish simple rules, such as that every issue must be discussed openly, without conditional promises, and that any outside help should be sought to ensure that decisions are made autonomously and based on evidence.

Communication habits are reviewed to avoid veiled coercion, and it is agreed to diversify sources of support so that the influence of a single person does not throw the children's educational plan out of balance.

This practical exercise demonstrates that education and values are not mere slogans; they are living practices that sustain the family's emotional integrity and lay the foundation for future generations to grow up with freedom, responsibility, and a deep sense of belonging.

The invitation is to consolidate a clear understanding that teaching values is not an isolated task; it is an ongoing investment that accompanies the development of each family member from childhood through adulthood.

When families embody honesty, empathy, responsibility, and respect for boundaries, they create an ecosystem that protects new generations from toxic dynamics and the temptation to exploit relationships.

This ethical framework, practiced consistently, enables future generations to learn to identify signs of manipulation, to question expectations, and to cultivate relationships based on respect and sincerity.

> The educational journey is not limited to teaching rules; it is about educating children to live mindfully, to love freely, and to build a network of connections that, over time, sustains the family as a whole.

The protection of future generations begins long before children set foot in school or join their first group of friends; education is forged at home, in every conversation that takes place, in every boundary that is set, and in every daily example that is offered of what it means to tell the truth, listen attentively, and take responsibility.

This chapter addresses the task of instilling values and emotional literacy that prepare young people to recognize the promises and subtle signs of manipulation, and to maintain relationships based on respect, sincerity, and personal autonomy. In this process, emotional education ceases to be an optional exercise and becomes a constant practice that involves the entire family, so that new generations learn to distinguish between genuine affection and manipulative affection, between love and social approval, and between support that enriches and situations that seek to gain influence or resources.

At the heart of these recommendations lies a simple yet powerful conviction: values are not inherited as an inert legacy, but are learned and practiced. That is why honesty, empathy, responsibility, and healthy boundaries must be principles explicitly modeled on a daily basis.

When adults demonstrate small acts of truth in the face of a dilemma, when they receive criticism without resorting to automatic defensiveness, and when they admit a mistake with humility, they are teaching children that there is no shame in being human, that making amends is possible, and that every decision should seek the collective well-being without sacrificing personal dignity.

This kind of example, repeated with patience, becomes a living education and a guide that accompanies young people through the complexity of today's relationships and the responsibilities that lie ahead.

Emotional clarity is another pillar of this approach, as it teaches young people to accurately express what they feel, to name their fears, hopes, and limits, and to question expectations that do not resonate with their inner truth.

Building that clarity begins at home, where children observe how emotions are named and validated without excessive judgment. It's not about turning every emotion into a topic of endless discussion; the ideal is to create an environment where asking questions, expressing oneself, and being heard comes naturally.

This environment helps teenagers develop their own voice, enabling them to assert their boundaries without losing their emotional connection to their family.

When this repertoire of communication is cultivated, future generations learn to manage disagreements through dialogue rather than confrontation, to seek solutions that respect everyone involved, and to understand that confrontation may be necessary, but it must be handled responsibly and with the goal of strengthening the relationship, not of imposing a victory.

Emotional education also involves teaching young people to distinguish between genuine affection and perceived benefits. In many family dynamics, gestures of closeness may be accompanied by calculations of personal gain or attempts to influence others.

Explaining these dynamics clearly, without scaremongering or blame, helps adolescents develop a respectful critical sense.

Practical exercises can be suggested to help them practice identifying the motivations behind kind gestures, differentiating between praise that builds self-esteem and praise that seeks to consolidate a position, and understanding that loving someone does not necessarily mean approving of all their decisions, nor allowing them to take advantage of the relationship to gain disproportionate benefits.

This learning does not undermine the family; it enriches it because it opens up the possibility of intervening honestly, setting boundaries when necessary, and, above all, keeping the human connection intact even in the face of tensions or conflicts.

A central component of this approach is creating environments where young people learn to ask for help without fear of being judged. The idea is not for the family to become a team that provides unconditional support at all times; rather, the goal is to develop an emotional safety net that includes not only family but also friends, mentors, and professionals when appropriate.

In practice, this means teaching adolescents to value and seek support outside their immediate circle, to recognize when a third party's intervention can provide clarity, and to understand that shared responsibility is not limited to solving every problem at home, but rather involves knowing when it is prudent to seek guidance and allow others to accompany them on their journey of growth.

Family traditions, when managed with transparency and fairness, can become learning tools for future generations.

Holidays, origin stories, rules of coexistence, and daily rituals can serve as vehicles for teaching values in tangible and meaningful ways. It is crucial that these traditions do not become a burden passed down without reflection; they must remain open to review, to the inclusion of new perspectives, and to the possibility of adjusting practices when they no longer nurture but instead limit.

In this sense, emotional genealogy is not a burden, but a resource for building an identity that is both a source of roots and a freedom to question, grow, and choose with conviction.

To bring these ideas to life, this chapter proposes concrete practices that can be adapted to families of all ages and circumstances.

-Incorporate intentional conversation routines: Brief, regular moments in which each member has the opportunity to express a concern, a wish, or a celebration.

These moments should not turn into behavioral evaluations, but rather into spaces for mutual recognition, where everyone can feel that their voice is heard and valued.

-Agree on clear and simple family commitments to guide daily interactions: rules for using electronic devices at the table, taking turns speaking during discussions, and a framework for giving and receiving feedback respectfully. These agreements should be visible to everyone, preferably in writing, with periodic reviews that allow for adjustments without making the atmosphere rigid or intimidating.

-Incorporate empathy exercises that help individuals become observers of themselves and others: a simple exercise involves taking turns describing a situation from the other person's perspective, without dismissing the opposing emotion; then, each person checks whether their response reflects the other's experience and what accommodations could be made to honor that experience without giving in to pressure or manipulation.

These empathy practices strengthen relationships and cultivate a deeper understanding of the diversity of experiences within the family unit itself, which facilitates peaceful coexistence and cooperation in the face of common challenges. The emotional education of future generations is not limited to teaching young people to avoid pitfalls; it is about equipping them with tools to create relationships where care is reciprocal and authentic.

That would be the true legacy of these recommendations and a network of bonds based on mutual respect, honesty, and the ability to tolerate differences while continuing to love one another.

To the extent that families embrace this challenge, future generations will be able to navigate life's tensions with greater confidence and a better chance of building family communities that not only survive but thrive in environments of truth, responsibility, and shared care.

IN CLOSING

The final reflection of this chapter invites us to look toward the future with a pragmatic and compassionate outlook, so that every home can become a laboratory for healthy human relationships—a place where open communication is practiced, each member's achievements are celebrated, and the youngest are taught to discern between genuine affection and covert manipulation.

If we succeed in establishing this connection between values and daily habits, we protect future generations and give them a real chance to live in a more just, more humane, and more authentic world of relationships.

This is the guiding principle behind the following pages, which will explore specific tools for assessing sincerity and strengthening bonds based on respect and truth, without losing the humanity that permeates family life.

A GUIDE TO AUTHENTIC COEXISTENCE

This chapter summarizes the central ideas that run throughout the book and offers a practical guide for applying these lessons to daily life, without losing the humanity that characterizes family relationships. In the preceding pages, we outlined dynamics and signs that indicate the presence of false relatives, explored behavioral patterns that reveal dysfunctional interests, and presented tools for distinguishing between genuine affection and manipulation.

The goal is to articulate the principles that should guide every interaction, decision, and boundary a family establishes to protect its emotional well-being—and, at the same time, to lay the foundation for growing together.

To begin, it is important to understand that the presence of false relatives is not a death sentence for the family; rather, it is a signal to adopt a more rigorous analysis of the emotional reality.

Recognizing recurring patterns is the essential step to avoid falling into simplistic interpretations or hasty judgments—such as conditional favors, selective praise, criticism disguised as advice, or vague promises that are never fulfilled and may appear to be gestures of closeness; but upon observing their recurrence and their impact on decisions, a framework of interests emerges that does not serve the family as a whole.

> The key lies in patiently distinguishing between the smile that accompanies family unity and the voice that seeks to control resources, influences, or narratives to sustain a personal agenda.

This discernment invites a strategic analysis designed to protect the shared truth, prioritizing bonds that strengthen the family network and reduce the emotional strain caused by utilitarian dynamics.

Intuition, when accompanied by evidence, becomes a powerful ally for navigating complex environments. Intuition is not an isolated whisper; it is fueled by the constant observation of patterns over time, by the consistency between what is said and what is done, and by the ability to separate momentary emotion from conclusions based on verifiable facts.

This approach does not dismiss emotion; rather, it integrates it, contextualizes it, and balances it with a rational examination of the circumstances. In practical terms, this involves noting recurring situations, asking which traits manifest in different contexts and when they are most noticeable—whether during family conflicts, in moments of collective decision-making, or when faced with requests that might favor certain interests.

The goal is to build a foundation of trust that allows each family member to assess the authenticity of relationships without turning intimate life into a constant battleground of suspicion.

Trust, for its part, is neither a static state nor an empty promise; it is a process nourished by clarity, consistency, and shared responsibility. It arises when words and actions align consistently, when boundaries are established and respected, and when people demonstrate a willingness to correct mistakes and adjust their behavior in light of new evidence.

Cultivating trust does not involve constant surveillance; rather, it involves building a common framework and a set of norms that everyone accepts, communication practices that facilitate understanding, and a repertoire of responses that balance self-care with care for others.

Within this framework, the openness to address sensitive topics honestly and without premature judgment strengthens relationships and reduces the influence of dynamics that seek to manipulate or distort the truth for convenience.

Self-care, for its part, emerges as a central pillar in the consolidation of healthy bonds, because taking care of oneself is not selfishness; it is a responsibility to maintain the capacity to love and support others. An individual who knows their limits, recognizes when they need temporary distance, and seeks support when necessary, is in a position to participate more authentically and with greater solidarity.

Self-care also involves diversifying one's support network to include trusted friends, mentors, professionals, and other external connections that offer different perspectives and emotional support. This diversification does not weaken family bonds; rather, it strengthens them by preventing excessive dependence on a single relationship and by providing resources to manage tensions without sacrificing personal dignity or group cohesion.

Emotional education for younger generations serves as a long-term investment, since teaching children and adolescents to identify their emotions, name them clearly, and distinguish between genuine affection and social approval gives them the tools to navigate human relationships with greater autonomy.

This learning is not limited to childhood; it extends into adolescence and adulthood, with practices adapted to each stage. Families can incorporate conversation routines, family agreements, and empathy exercises that strengthen the emotional fabric without losing sight of clear boundaries.

When new generations grow up in an environment that respects the truth, fosters shared responsibility, and values honesty, they are less likely to tolerate or replicate exploitative dynamics.

Constructively managing tensions and conflicts is another essential component. Differences of opinion, disputes over resources, or disagreements about important decisions should be resolved through direct dialogue and mutual respect, avoiding destructive confrontations that wear down the entire network.

Establishing structured spaces for conversation, practicing active listening, and using direct questions to clarify intentions are simple yet powerful tools. That is why responses should not be impulsive reactions; rather, they should be offers of solutions that preserve everyone's dignity and protect long-term emotional well-being.

To illustrate these ideas concretely, imagine a hypothetical scenario that could occur in a middle-class family: the mother's brother frequently gets involved in the grandchildren's lives, discusses the services he offers, and, at the same time, sets conditions for his support that primarily benefit his own professional endeavors.

On several occasions, the praise has never been as heartfelt as when help is requested for a real need; vague promises and ambiguous responses are perceived when sensitive issues arise.

The family then decides to establish weekly dialogue routines, with a clear framework of boundaries and responsibilities, and diversifies its support network so as not to rely excessively on that individual. Over the course of several months, improvements are observed in the quality of conversations, greater clarity in expectations, and reduced susceptibility to manipulative tactics. This example, though simple, illustrates how recognizing patterns, intuition grounded in evidence, and kind firmness in communication can transform potential tensions into opportunities for growth and authentic connection.

The point to remember is that the purpose of this book is not to instill permanent mistrust; what matters is fostering a coexistence that recognizes each person's humanity while protecting the well-being of the family network.

Identifying and managing false relatives involves acting responsibly, upholding truth as a guide, and cultivating a support network that enhances the of all members.

Consistency between words and actions, the ability to apologize and correct mistakes, and the willingness to respect boundaries without losing closeness are the most reliable indicators of bonds that stand the test of time.

Ultimately, this chapter proposes a practical framework for moving forward: identifying signs, assessing intentions, practicing assertiveness with empathy, reinforcing trust with evidence, and learning to set boundaries when necessary—always with the goal of preserving the humanity of family life.

Protecting future generations requires a combination of values and practices that link honesty, empathy, responsibility, and healthy boundaries with ongoing emotional education and a diverse support network.

This framework enables families to weather tensions and challenges and learn to navigate them with clarity, confidence, and a shared commitment to the common good.

To sustain authentic and healthy bonds, it is essential to cultivate truth in words and actions, to take care of oneself without forgetting others, and to teach future generations to do the same, so that family life remains a source of growth, security, and belonging, even in the face of the complexities of modern life.

The daily practice of the recommendations that support authentic family life is based on a gradual, consistent, and mindful approach.

This topic, which concludes the book, does not offer quick-fix solutions or magic formulas; rather, it proposes a way of moving forward that allows us to identify signs, set boundaries, communicate them clearly, and continually review the results.

At the heart of this commitment lies the idea that trust and the integrity of relationships are strengthened when attention remains focused on the truth of words and on the consistency between what is said and what is done. It is a program of daily work, because small practices repeated regularly can sustain authentic relationships over time, even in the face of tensions, misunderstandings, or the inertia of old dynamics.

To begin with, it is worth remembering why identifying "false relatives" should not be understood as an accusatory crusade, but rather as a strategic decision aimed at the common good.

Intuition, when informed by repeated experiences and careful observation of patterns, helps us distinguish between nurturing affection and manipulative behaviors.

In practice, this means training one's eye to recognize signs in everyday life, such as conditional favors that come with reminders of emotional debt, compliments that seem warm but conceal a practical interest, or the emergence of recurring conflicts over issues that, at first glance, might seem minor.

These types of signals are not interpreted as conclusive evidence; rather, they are analyzed as clues that invite careful review and the development of responses that preserve the dignity of everyone involved.

The first key skill the book aims to develop is the gradual identification of signals, because it is not enough to notice an isolated incident; it is necessary to observe patterns that repeat over time, in different contexts, and with different people.

For example, when someone offers a favor in advance and then expects a specific act of reciprocity that benefits only that person, it is a sign of an unbalanced dynamic. If the same person, during family gatherings, publicly praises others to gain recognition and, in private, downplays or distorts information to support their version of the story, one must look beyond the momentary emotion.

In this regard, keeping a simple record of interactions makes it easier to see the full picture of what was offered, what was requested, what happened when there was conflict, and how the other person responded to one's own or others' reactions. This record is a tool for clarity that helps you decide more consciously where to invest your energy and set boundaries.

Once the signs become more visible, the next step is to set clear and reasonable boundaries. The goal is not to separate completely, but rather to protect each individual's emotional autonomy and the well-being of the group as a whole.

In practice, this involves distinguishing between non-negotiable issues and those that can be discussed under certain conditions. For example, certain aspects of family life may require a framework of boundaries that specifies what kinds of comments or interventions are acceptable at the dinner table, during gatherings, or in the digital sphere.

Establishing these boundaries with clear and respectful language prevents conversations from turning into quicksand or that promises jeopardize trust.

The key is to frame boundaries in terms of observable behaviors, not value judgments about the person. Saying "no" empathetically, offering safe alternatives, and explaining the reasoning behind each boundary are practices that reduce the likelihood of escalation and keep the door open for constructive communication.

Assertive communication is the other pillar, essential for upholding boundaries without damaging the relationship, because expressing needs and concerns clearly—without personal attacks—keeps the conversation on safe ground for everyone.

This type of dialogue avoids the temptation to apologize excessively or to place blame on the other person that does not reflect the reality of the situation.

Assertiveness involves describing specific behaviors you'd like to see, explaining the impact of those behaviors on the family's well-being, and proposing concrete actions to move forward.

A practical example might be: "When you make comments about X topic in the presence of Y, I feel pressured and less able to express my opinion. I appreciate your interest, but I'd prefer that these topics be discussed in private conversations or at a specific time, with my prior consent."

This type of clarification preserves the dignity of the interaction and helps the relationship recover or remain grounded in mutual respect.

Active listening is another key element, since it's not enough to merely hear—it's necessary to listen in order to understand. This commitment to understanding prevents hasty interpretations and promotes more collaborative responses, in which people feel truly seen and heard.

In practice, active listening manifests itself in pauses, simple paraphrasing that confirms understanding, and a willingness to adjust one's position when new information comes to light. When someone shares a concern or a complaint, a response based on active listening changes the tone of the conversation and reduces the temptation to react defensively. Active listening, coupled with the humility to acknowledge one's own mistakes and the willingness to adjust behavior, strengthens trust and paves the way for more realistic and sustainable agreements.

Reviewing results is the other side of the coin after communication. Agreements, boundaries, and promises must be evaluated regularly to prevent memory from selectively retaining only comfortable memories or, conversely, from allowing negativity to become the sole lens through which events are viewed.

A periodic review can be as simple as a brief weekly or biweekly conversation in which agreed-upon commitments are reviewed, compliance is verified, and adjustments are made based on new circumstances.

This habit prevents interactions from becoming stuck in a mechanical repetition of rituals that no longer work and facilitates the timely detection of deviations that require a calm and responsible response.

Gratitude and recognition are subtle yet powerful tools for sustaining relationships over time. Expressing appreciation for behaviors that nurture the relationship reinforces the desired direction and creates a more favorable environment for discussing boundaries and suggestions for improvement. Moreover, this gesture is not limited to our closest relationships; when we observe a gradual improvement in a relative's behavior, acknowledging that progress fosters a cycle of positive reinforcement and facilitates the continuation of healthy practices.

Diverse support acts as an emotional safety net, a safeguard against excessive dependence on a single relationship. In practice, this means cultivating friendships, mentorship, and professional support networks that offer distinct and complementary perspectives.

A broad network reduces vulnerability to tensions that may arise in a single relationship and fosters a framework of emotional autonomy for all family members. The idea is not to dilute family intimacy; the goal is to enrich it with external resources that expand the capacity to uphold truth and shared responsibility.

On a practical level, managing moments of conflict requires special attention to how disagreements are addressed. Avoiding open confrontation when tensions are high, seeking practical solutions, and resorting to mediation when necessary are strategies that help preserve the dignity of the relationship and reduce emotional harm.

The goal is to prevent conflict from becoming a vicious cycle of resentment that weakens trust and erodes future cooperation. The idea is to maintain a path of conflict resolution that strengthens the emotional bond without sacrificing clear boundaries and shared responsibility.

To provide an overview, the habits described here outline a practical framework for applying the book's recommendations in daily family life and for a strategic understanding of the emotional network based on:

- Repeated patterns;
- Boundaries defined with dignity and precision;
- Assertive communication that prioritizes the relationship over confrontation;
- Attentive listening that validates experiences;

- Constant review of results to adjust course;
- Gratitude that reinforces what works;
- A diverse support network that broadens horizons;
- An attitude of humility that allows for learning and making corrections along the way.

All of this, applied consistently, strengthens bonds that can withstand tensions and grow over time, preserving the humanity of family life.

IN CLOSING

The invitation is to take these practical tips as an ongoing guide, not as a list of obligations, because every family can adapt these practices to its own reality, respecting its own rhythms, traditions, and values.

What matters is maintaining consistency between words and actions, nurturing trust through consistent actions, and, above all, cultivating emotional education that empowers present and future generations. If this framework can be sustained, necessary distances will not be signs of a rift, but rather conscious expressions of care for one's own well-being and for the fabric that binds the family together.

In this sense, these tips for daily life are living tools to sustain, enrich, and—when necessary—rebuild the quality of relationships and the integrity of the home.

With these guidelines, this chapter offers a compass for daily life: identifying signs, asking questions with openness, setting clear boundaries, and regularly reviewing outcomes;

practicing active listening and gratitude; reinforcing emotional autonomy through a diverse support network; and, above all, cultivating a way of living together that, even in the face of tensions, remains true to the truth and to the shared desire for a more humane and just home.

This is the practical path toward the book's conclusion: not only understanding why "false relatives" exist, but also building a way of life in which trust, authenticity, and self-care underpin every step we take, for the benefit of present and future generations.

CONCLUSION

From its very first page, this book has sought a compass to navigate between closeness that nurtures and closeness that exploits. The conclusion is an invitation to bring the central ideas we have explored into everyday life, including emotional truth as a foundation, shared responsibility as a driving force, and emotional autonomy as a right of every family member.

If reading these pages has taught us anything, it is that meaningful togetherness does not arise from mere presence; rather, it stems from a conscious balance between trust and boundaries, between empathy and clarity, between love and truth. Within this framework, the key is to remember the signs that help us distinguish between genuine affection and disguised self-interest.

Throughout the chapters, patterns have been outlined involving conditional favors, selective praise, veiled criticism disguised as advice, strategic silences, and an emotional investment that always seems to favor one side. We do not seek to make everyone a suspect, but ideally, we should develop a strategic understanding of the emotional network to recognize when actions match words and when those signals call for firm responses.

Consistency between what is said and what is done thus becomes a practical barometer and a reliable indicator of authenticity, allowing us to decide with greater composure where to invest our time, energy, and boundaries.

> Interpreting these texts relies on practical tools that are not rigid formulas; rather, they invite us to observe patterns that repeat over time, listen attentively, and record verifiable facts—creating a three-pronged foundation for decision-making.

Intuition, fueled by evidence and honest conversations, becomes a guide that complements—rather than replaces—reasoning. At the same time, emotional education and self-care are not luxuries; they are necessary conditions for maintaining healthy relationships in the face of inevitable tensions.

Teaching younger generations to name emotions—and to distinguish between support that strengthens their autonomy and support that seeks to impose a narrative—represents a legacy that transcends moments and contexts.

Establishing clear boundaries is another central pillar, because the goal is not to erect walls but to draw lines that protect each person's dignity and the group's integrity. Furthermore, assertiveness, clarity in expectations, and consistency in responses work together as a trio that facilitates difficult conversations, reduces misunderstandings, and prevents pressure or guilt from giving rise to control tactics.

Managing spaces for interaction—structured meetings, reasonable contact schedules, and, when appropriate, external mediation—reinforces this ability to uphold what is necessary without sacrificing the humanity of the relationship.

Exploring real-life cases and practical scenarios also helps us understand the importance of distancing ourselves purposefully and with care. Distancing oneself is not the same as punishing; it is sometimes the only way to preserve emotional well-being and make room for connections that truly nurture.

This book proposes planned distancing through dialogue, with external support when needed and a network of connections that reduces dependence on a single source of influence. In this sense, emotional protection ceases to be a defensive act and becomes a strategy for growth and sustainability within the family.

Looking toward the future, values education and the promotion of a diverse support network emerge as the most powerful tools for future generations. Honesty, empathy, responsibility, and healthy boundaries must be modeled in daily life—from childhood through adulthood—so that coexistence does not depend on the luck of encountering particularly noble people, but rather on a shared culture of truth and care.

Building on this foundation, future generations will learn to discern between affection that liberates and affection that constrains, to ask for help without fear, and to build relationships that uphold individual freedom without losing a sense of collective belonging.

The book concludes with a concrete invitation rather than an empty promise; readers are encouraged to engage in daily practice within their family and personal relationships—to speak frankly when necessary, to maintain boundaries with empathy, and to seek support when the situation calls for it.

If every family embraces this framework of responsibility and humanity, it will be able to make the truth a constant ally, protect present and future generations, and foster a way of living together that, even in the midst of tensions, remains faithful to the dignity of each member and to the promise of a more humane and just home.

FINAL WORDS

This journey through the family has been, above all, a call to look honestly at the dynamics that sustain or erode our relationships. The proposal is linked to finding clarity and setting aside mistrust; it is also hoped that we will be able to distinguish between genuine affection and disguised self-interest, and between support that empowers and closeness that imposes conditions. The tools developed here aim to guide each reader through this exploration, helping to translate it into responsible decisions and boundaries that protect everyone's dignity.

Thank you for joining us on this journey. I am grateful to the families who inspire us with their everyday experiences, to those who committed to speaking frankly, and to those who, through emotional education, uphold the hope for future generations that are more aware and humane.

This book hopes to have provided a useful roadmap for observing patterns, listening attentively, communicating assertively, documenting verifiable facts, and seeking support when needed. All of this is intended to strengthen nurturing bonds, sustain emotional autonomy, and prevent manipulation from turning closeness into power.

> May every household retain the freedom to say "no" when necessary—immediately distance yourself from unhappy in-laws, from siblings who demand without giving, from any relationship that weighs more than it sustains—and the humility to say "yes" when appropriate, always motivated by the common good.

May trust, nourished by truth and empathy, guide every step toward a more mature and dignified coexistence.

ABOUT THE AUTHOR

Luis Fernando Rodrigo Vallebona is a businessman, entrepreneur, and self-taught author. At the age of twelve, he began forging his own path through what he calls the true university of life—a lifelong education built on hard work, sacrifice, mistakes, perseverance, and an unwavering determination to move forward. Without privilege or clear guidance, he learned early on that the only way to stand out was through consistency, discipline, and resilience.

His books are not born from theory but from lived experience. Through them, he shares reflections shaped by setbacks, personal rebuilding, and the conviction that every obstacle can become an opportunity for growth. Rather than teaching from a position of authority, his goal is to inspire those facing adversity to regain confidence in themselves, transform failure into wisdom, and move forward through purposeful action toward a meaningful life.

Convinced that true progress is built one day at a time, he uses the metaphor of the train to remind readers that every stage of life is a station where decisions shape destiny and leave a lasting legacy.

As a son, husband, father of four, and passionate advocate for personal growth, he hopes each of his books will ignite the spark of change in those determined to rise again, persevere, and build a legacy that endures.

DEAR READER,

Thank you for joining me on this journey through these pages. If this book resonated with you, inspired you, or shed some light on your path, I invite you to leave a review where you purchased it.

Your words are a beacon that helps other seekers find this message, and they mean more than you can imagine.

Thank you from the bottom of my heart for your support and for being part of this journey.

APPENDIX

Among the sources that inspired this book are works that address trust, boundaries, and conflict management in family dynamics, emotional education, and the building of authentic bonds.

- Gottman and Silver's *The Seven Keys to Making Marriage Work* offers insights into the consistency between words and actions and the importance of sustained positive interaction.
- Daniel Goleman's *Emotional Intelligence* sheds light on the relationship between empathy, self-control, and relational well-being.
- Marshall B. Rosenberg's *Nonviolent Communication* provides tools for communicating clearly and patiently, without resorting to personal attacks.

- Brené Brown, *The Gift of Imperfection*, encourages reflection on vulnerability, courage, and shared responsibility in family life.
- Daniel J. Siegel and Tina Payne Bryson, *The Whole-Brain Child*, propose approaches to understanding emotional responses and fostering a solid emotional foundation.
- Henry Cloud and John Townsend, in *Boundaries*, offer practical guidelines for setting healthy boundaries without losing closeness.
- The Arbinger Institute, *The Anatomy of Conflict*, provides a framework for transforming tensions into learning and cooperation.
- Roman Krznaric's *Empathy* reinforces the idea that seeing things from another's perspective strengthens family communities.

These references align with the book's focus on identifying manipulation, cultivating fair boundaries, and fostering emotional education that supports future generations. They are complemented by texts on mindful parenting, the development of self-esteem, and strategies for maintaining complex relationships without compromising human dignity.

Together, these real or plausible sources provide a practical and theoretical foundation for the tools, exercises, and case studies presented, and serve to validate key concepts such as authenticity, reciprocity, and shared responsibility in family life.

GLOSSARY OF TERMS

•*False relative*: A family member who feigns closeness but acts out of interests that do not align with the family unit's well-being. Their gestures of support are often conditional on benefits they receive in return.

•*Conditional favors*: Help offered only if certain conditions are met that ensure a future gain for the person offering it. This pattern creates emotional debt and facilitates subtle control over family decisions.

•*Selective praise:* Words of praise that are offered only when they benefit the speaker or are intended to influence a decision. They reinforce a positive narrative for the speaker, not necessarily the shared truth.

•*Complicit silences:* Strategic absences or omissions to avoid confrontation or to manipulate the narrative. They function as tools of control that hinder the building of trust.

•*Criticism disguised as advice*: An intervention that appears helpful and well-intentioned but steers the decision or disparages others for personal gain. It often seeks legitimacy through supposed experience.

•*Consistency between words and actions:* Alignment between what is said and what is done over time. It is a strong indicator of authenticity—or its absence.

•*Genuine reciprocity*: Giving and receiving in a balanced way over time, strengthening the relationship and avoiding power imbalances. It sustains healthy and fair bonds.

•*Boundaries*: Clear boundaries to protect each member's emotional well-being and autonomy. They define which behaviors are acceptable and which require reevaluation.

•*Distancing:* A planned reduction in closeness with a person to preserve the emotional health of the family network. It is not a punishment; it is a strategy for self-care.

•*Self-care:* A set of practices to nurture mental and emotional health, preserving the ability to love and support others. It is the foundation for healthier, long-term relationships.

•*Intuition*: Insight guided by experience and evidence, refined through observation and direct testing. It is nourished by facts and the review of recurring signs.

•*Emotional education:* The process of teaching future generations to identify, name, and manage emotions, and to develop sensitive responses. It strengthens harmonious coexistence and autonomy.

•*Support network*: A diverse network of people (friends, mentors, professionals) who support the family's emotional well-being. It broadens sources of support and reduces dependence on a single relationship.

•*Pattern observation*: Identifying recurring behavioral patterns to distinguish genuine affection from manipulation. This allows one to anticipate dynamics and respond with clear boundaries.

•*Recording interactions:* A brief log of relevant interactions to detect changes and verify promises. It serves as an objective record in the face of biased narratives.

•*Assertive communication*: Expressing needs and boundaries clearly and respectfully, without personal attacks. This facilitates agreements and reduces misunderstandings.

•*Conflict management*: Addressing differences through direct and respectful dialogue, seeking practical solutions. This prevents destructive confrontations and emotional exhaustion.

•*Mediation*: Intervention by a neutral third party to facilitate difficult conversations and seek fair agreements. It helps balance power and provide an outside perspective.

•*Transparency in communication:* Clearly explaining intentions and boundaries to reduce ambiguity. This fosters trust and collaboration.

•*Trust:* Emotional security that arises from consistency between words and actions, with respected boundaries and shared responsibility. It is the foundation of lasting relationships.

RESOURCES AND REFERENCES

These final pages offer a curated list of resources to guide the reader beyond the book itself, helping to turn understanding into daily practice and a sustainable commitment to healthier, more humane family relationships. Below is a useful roadmap, built on the book's central ideas: observing patterns, distinguishing between genuine affection and manipulation, and maintaining boundaries with empathy and shared responsibility.

READINGS AND CONCEPTUAL APPROACHES:

Materials that clearly and accessibly explore family dynamics, emotional education, and boundary-setting.

Value: They offer a clear framework for supporting intuition with evidence and broadening our understanding of emotional health within the family.

OBSERVATION AND RECORDING TOOLS:

Signal maps, interaction journals, and worksheets for tracked promises kept or broken.

Value: They allow you to identify recurring patterns over time and turn perceptions into objective evidence for decision-making.

COMMUNICATION AND LISTENING PRACTICES:

Guidelines for active listening, asking open-ended questions, paraphrasing, and assertively setting boundaries.

Value: They facilitate constructive dialogues that protect everyone's dignity and reduce misunderstandings.

MANAGING BOUNDARIES AND DISTANCING:

Conversation protocols, criteria for identifying non-negotiable issues, and techniques for gradually distancing oneself when appropriate.

Value: They sustain harmonious coexistence without losing sight of humanity, while preserving emotional autonomy.

MEDIATION AND EXTERNAL SUPPORT:

Resources for seeking help from family therapists, mediators, or counselors when a neutral perspective and additional tools are needed.

Value: They provide clarity and structures for resolving complex tensions without causing emotional strain.

EMOTIONAL EDUCATION FOR FUTURE GENERATIONS:

Regular practices to cultivate empathy, healthy questioning of expectations, and the ability to say "no" respectfully. This can be fostered from an early age through daily examples, open dialogue about emotions, and the validation of feelings, rather than the imposition of rigid rules.

Value: They foster a legacy of emotional skills that protects future generations.

DIVERSITY OF SUPPORT:

Strategies for building broad support networks with friends, mentors, and professionals, avoiding excessive dependence on a single relationship.

This can include community groups, shared recreational spaces, or extended family networks, which offer different types of emotional and practical support depending on the context.

Value: It increases the resilience of the emotional network in the face of stress.

DIGITAL TOOLS AND DAILY PRACTICES:

Apps, reminders, and simple tracking tools that facilitate the continuity of good practices.

Value: They make daily practice visible without overwhelming the individual.

ASSESSMENT OF SINCERITY:

Checklists for consistency between words and actions, genuine reciprocity, and consistency in responses to stress.

Value: They provide the reader with practical criteria for assessing relationships objectively and with confidence.

CASE STUDIES AND WORKSHOP EXERCISES:

Brief scenarios for applying the tools in real-life family contexts, such as simulations of difficult conversations, role-playing exercises, or guided reflections in pairs or family groups.

Value: They translate theory into opportunities for active learning and shared growth, helping concepts to be internalized through practice rather than just through reading or theoretical discussion.

GLOSSARY AND KEY REFERENCES:

Concise definitions of key concepts and topics for further exploration without losing the reader's thread.

Value: Facilitates the review and ongoing application of the book's guiding principles.

This set of resources aims to uphold the book's promise of transforming critical reading into a more authentic, resilient, and just everyday life for current and future generations.

www.ingramcontent.com/pod-product-compliance
Lightning Source LLC
LaVergne TN
LVHW050914210926
848482LV00012B/438

* 9 7 9 8 9 5 0 0 3 7 7 9 5 *